Golden Nuggets

from Forgotten Places

SELECTED STUDIES FROM KINGS AND CHRONICLES

From the Bible-teaching ministry of

Charles R. Swindoll

INSIGHT FOR LIVING

Chuck graduated in 1963 from Dallas Theological Seminary, where he now serves as the school's fourth president, helping to prepare a new generation of men and women for the ministry. Chuck has served in pastorates in three states: Massachusetts, Texas, and California, including almost twenty-three years at the First Evangelical Free Church in Fullerton, California. His sermon messages have been aired over radio since 1979 as the *Insight for Living* broadcast. A best-selling author, Chuck has written numerous books and booklets on many subjects.

Based on the outlines and transcripts of Chuck's sermons, the study guide text is co-authored by Gary Matlack, a graduate of Texas Tech University and Dallas Theological Seminary. He also wrote the Living Insights sections.

Editor in Chief:
Cynthia Swindoll

Coauthor of Text:
Gary Matlack

Assistant Editor and Writer:
Wendy Peterson

Copy Editors:
Tom Kimber
Marco Salazar

Cover Designer:
Nina Paris

Text Designer:
Gary Lett

Graphics System Administrator:
Bob Haskins

Publishing System Specialist:
Alex Pasieka

Director, Communications Division:
Deedee Snyder

Marketing Manager:
Alene Cooper

Project Coordinator:
Colette Muse

Production Manager:
John Norton

Unless otherwise identified, all Scripture references are from the New American Standard Bible, © The Lockman Foundation 1960, 1962, 1963, 1968, 1971, 1972, 1973, 1975, 1977. Used by permission. Scripture taken from the Holy Bible, New International Version © 1973, 1978, 1984 International Bible Society, used by permission of Zondervan Bible Publishers.

CONTENTS

INTRODUCTION

Believe it or not, some people consider the historical books of Kings and Chronicles to be the wasteland of the Bible—vast, unsightly, strewn with hard-to-pronounce names and endless, boring genealogies. Wrong!

Actually, Kings and Chronicles are more like a mine, rich in spiritual insights and glittering with nuggets of practical truth. Maybe it's been a while since you did any digging in these books. If so, grab a pick and come along. We'll unearth some timeless treasures and learn afresh that God's Word never loses its value.

Chuck Swindoll

PUTTING TRUTH INTO ACTION

K nowledge apart from application falls short of God's desire for His children. He wants us to apply what we learn so that we will change and grow. This study guide was prepared with these goals in mind. As you go through the following pages, we hope your desire to discover biblical truth will grow as your understanding of God's Word increases and that you will be encouraged to apply what you've learned.

To assist you in your study, we've included a section called Living Insights at the end of each lesson. These exercises will challenge you to study further and to think of specific ways to put your discoveries into action.

On occasion a lesson is followed by a Digging Deeper section, which gives you additional information and resources to probe further into some issues raised in that lesson.

There are many ways to use this guide—in personal devotions, group studies, discussions with friends and family, and Sunday school classes. And, of course, it's an ideal study aid when you're listening to its corresponding *Insight for Living* radio series.

To benefit most from this study guide, we would encourage you to consider it a spiritual journal. That's why we've included space in the Living Insights for recording your thoughts and discoveries. We hope you'll return to those sections often for review and encouragement as you continue to grow in your walk with Christ.

Gary Matlack
Coauthor of Text
Author of Living Insights

Golden Nuggets

from Forgotten Places

SELECTED STUDIES FROM KINGS AND CHRONICLES

THE KINGS AND PROPHETS
THE NORTHERN KINGDOM: ISRAEL 931–722 B.C.

Prophets	Kings	Godly?	Years Reigned	Scripture Record
	Jeroboam I	No	22	1 Kings 12–14
	Nadab	No	2	1 Kings 15
	Baasha	No	24	1 Kings 15–16
	Elah	No	2	1 Kings 16
	Zimri	No	7 days	1 Kings 16
	Omri[1]	No	12	1 Kings 16
Elijah	Ahab	No	22	1 Kings 16–22
Elijah	Ahaziah	No	2	1 Kings 22; 2 Kings 1
Elijah	Jehoram (Joram)	No	12	2 Kings 3–8
Elisha	Jehu	No	28	2 Kings 9–10
Elisha	Jehoahaz (Joahaz)	No	17	2 Kings 13
Elisha	Jehoash (Joash)	No	16	2 Kings 13
Jonah / Amos	Jeroboam II	No	41	2 Kings 14
Hosea	Zechariah	No	6 months	2 Kings 15
Hosea	Shallum	No	1 month	2 Kings 15
Hosea	Menahem	No	10	2 Kings 15
Hosea	Pekahiah	No	2	2 Kings 15
Hosea	Pekah	No	20	2 Kings 15
Hosea	Hoshea	No	9	2 Kings 17

ASSYRIAN CAPTIVITY: 722 B.C.

The kings of both Israel and Judah are listed in the order of their reigns. Since Scripture refers to some kings by more than one name, alternate names are given in parentheses. The prophets' names appear in boxes to show which prophets ministered under which kings. Not all the prophets are mentioned, only the better known ones.

1. Some commentators consider Tibni, who fought with Omri for the throne, a legitimate king. That would bring the count of Israel's kings to twenty.

* Charts adapted from John F. Walvoord and Roy B. Zuck, eds., *The Bible Knowledge Commentary*, Old Testament edition (Wheaton, Ill.: Scripture Press Publications, Victor Books, 1985), p. 513.

The Kings and Prophets
The Southern Kingdom: Judah 931–586 B.C.

Kings	Godly?	Years Reigned	Scripture Record
Rehoboam	No	17	1 Kings 12–14; 2 Chron. 11–12
Abijah (Abijam)	No	3	1 Kings 15; 2 Chron. 13
Asa	Yes	41	1 Kings 15; 2 Chron. 14–16
Jehoshaphat	Yes	25	1 Kings 22; 2 Chron. 17–20
Jehoram *Obadiah*	No	8	2 Kings 8; 2 Chron. 21
Ahaziah	No	1	2 Kings 8; 2 Chron. 22
Queen Athaliah	No	6	2 Kings 11; 2 Chron. 22–23
Joash (Jehoash) *Joel*	Yes	40	2 Kings 12–13; 2 Chron. 24
Amaziah	Yes	29	2 Kings 14; 2 Chron. 25
Uzziah (Azariah)	Yes	52	2 Kings 15; 2 Chron. 26
Jotham	Yes	16	2 Kings 15; 2 Chron. 27
Ahaz	No	16	2 Kings 16; 2 Chron. 28; Isa. 7–12
Hezekiah	Yes	29	2 Kings 18–20; 2 Chron. 29–32; Isa. 36–39
Manasseh *Nahum*	No	55	2 Kings 21; 2 Chron. 33
Amon	No	2	2 Kings 21; 2 Chron. 33
Josiah *Zephaniah*	Yes	31	2 Kings 22–23; 2 Chron. 34–35
Jehoahaz (Joahaz)	No	3 months	2 Kings 23; 2 Chron. 36
Jehoiakim *Habakkuk*	No	11	2 Kings 23–24; 2 Chron. 36
Jehoiachin	No	3 months	2 Kings 24; 2 Chron. 36
Zedekiah	No	11	2 Kings 24–25; 2 Chron. 36; Jer. 52

(Left margin spanning brackets: Micah, Isaiah, Jeremiah)

Babylonian Captivity: 586 B.C.

Exilic Prophets: Daniel, Ezekiel, Jeremiah (Lamentations)

Postexilic Prophets: Haggai, Zechariah, Malachi

Chapter 1

DIG . . . AND YOU
SHALL FIND

A Historical Survey of Kings and Chronicles

A gold mine is nothing more
than a hole in the ground owned by a liar.
—Mark Twain

Looks like Mark Twain might have been sold a bill of goods once
or twice in his day. Maybe he had to learn the hard way that
some treasures are illusory, that many things glitter from a distance
but lose their luster up close, that some promises fail to deliver,
fading like an echo in an abandoned mine shaft.

Perhaps Twain would have been encouraged by the authentic
treasure found by another seeker, King Solomon of Israel:

How blessed is the man who finds wisdom,
And the man who gains understanding.
For its profit is better than the profit of silver,
And its gain than fine gold.
She is more precious than jewels;
And nothing you desire compares with her.
(Prov. 3:13–15)

The wisdom tucked away in God's Word—now *there's* treasure.
And it's right under our noses. It always delivers what it promises.
It always increases in value. It never runs out.

Unfortunately, many Christians haven't dug deep enough to
discover the bounty buried in the pages of Scripture. Many are con-
tent to stuff a couple of nuggets in their pockets, when wheelbarrows-
full are waiting to be hauled out and deposited in the vaults of their
hearts. There's nothing wrong with polishing and admiring such
familiar passages as John 3:16 and the Twenty-third Psalm. But
there's so much more to discover.

1

Many of us have hardly disturbed the soil above some scriptural treasures. Take 1 and 2 Kings and 1 and 2 Chronicles, for example. Many Christians walk right by these books for fear of falling into a maze of long genealogies, hard-to-pronounce names, and miscellaneous skirmishes.

But running through these historical books is a mother lode of spiritual truth. Here you'll find God's holiness and righteous judgment. His forbearing love for sinful humanity. The price of disobedience. The preservation of His covenant people through all kinds of adversity. God's sovereignty over nations and kings, godly and pagan. And much more.

All Scripture was given to us by God for our spiritual enrichment (Rom. 15:4; 2 Tim. 3:16), including Kings and Chronicles. What we need to do is search for it, as Solomon advised:

> My son, if you will receive my sayings,
> And treasure my commandments within you,
> Make your ear attentive to wisdom,
> Incline your heart to understanding;
> For if you cry for discernment,
> Lift your voice for understanding;
> If you seek her as silver,
> And search for her as for hidden treasures;
> Then you will discern the fear of the Lord,
> And discover the knowledge of God.
> (Prov. 2:1–5)

Excited? Then grab a pick and let's start digging. And don't forget your wheelbarrow!

A Tale of Two Kingdoms

Sadly, Kings and Chronicles recount a kingdom divided—severed into two separate kingdoms by the jagged blade of God's judgment. During this time of division, both kingdoms were characterized by disobedience and idol worship. And both kingdoms were eventually judged by God and taken into captivity by pagan nations.[1]

---

1. The books of Kings go from David's death through the histories of both Israel and Judah. The Chronicles, though, start with genealogies, then follow David's line—from the start of his reign to the captivity of Judah. The Chronicles offer a more spiritually oriented commentary on Judah's history.

An Identity Crisis

So how did Israel get into this mess? Remember, first of all, that Israel existed as a unified nation for 120 years under Saul, David, and Solomon (see Acts 13:21[2]; 2 Sam. 5:4–5; 1 Kings 11:42). Then Solomon, whom God had blessed with more wealth and wisdom than any other man, turned away from God to worship idols (see 1 Kings 11:4–10). And so "the king with the divided heart [left] behind a divided kingdom."[3]

After Solomon's death in 931 B.C., his son Rehoboam became king of Israel. But the twelve-tribe kingdom didn't hold together long, as God had already predicted (see vv. 11–13, 29–39). Jeroboam, a former subordinate of Solomon, rebelled and took ten tribes with him. Jeroboam, then, became king over the northern kingdom—Israel. Rehoboam ruled over the remaining two tribes in the south, which together made up the nation of Judah (see 12:12–20).

Israel, the northern kingdom, consisted of ten tribes. Its capital moved from Shechem to Tirzah and finally to Samaria. Judah, the southern kingdom, consisted of two tribes. Its capital was Jerusalem. These distinctions are important when reading through Kings and Chronicles. They'll help us keep our kings, battles, invasions, and prophets straight.

A Collision Course

So from Solomon's death onward, we have two nations, both on a collision course with captivity. The northern kingdom will fall to the Assyrians 209 years later in 722 B.C. The southern kingdom will exist 345 years, finally falling to the Babylonians in 586 B.C. History flatters neither nation. The prevailing characteristic of both Israel and Judah is disobedience. Yet in the midst of flagrant idolatry and immorality, God still preserves and ministers to His people.

2. In the NASB, 1 Samuel 13:1 gives the duration of Saul's reign as thirty-two years. But Acts 13:21 says he reigned for forty years. This discrepancy is due to the Masoretic text, which has lost the number that must have been included in the original Hebrew manuscript. It seems best, as Gleason Archer suggests, to render 1 Samuel 13:1 as "And he had ruled two years over Israel when he chose out for himself . . ." The text allows for this interpretation, which focuses on how long Saul had reigned before the events described in 1 Samuel 13 rather than Saul's overall reign. We can assume, then, that his reign actually lasted forty years, as Acts 13:21 says. For more information on these verses, see Gleason Archer's *Encyclopedia of Bible Difficulties* (Grand Rapids, Mich.: Regency Reference Library, Zondervan Publishing House, 1916), pp. 171–172.

3. Bruce Wilkinson and Kenneth Boa, *Talk Thru the Old Testament*, vol. 1 of *Talk Thru the Bible* (Nashville, Tenn.: Thomas Nelson Publishers, 1983), p. 84.

Prophets and Kings . . . and "Things"

The chart at the front of the guide will help you organize the people and events in these four historical books. Notice that Israel was ruled by nineteen kings, every one of them bad. Judah fared a little better—eight out of twenty of her monarchs are classified as good. To these disobedient rulers and the people they ruled, God sent His prophets to confront their wickedness and call them back to Himself.

Who Were the Big Names?

Let's look at a few of the players from this stage of history. Notice, first of all, the variation in the length of time the kings reigned. Manasseh of Judah ruled the longest, fifty-five years. Zimri, on the other hand, ruled Israel for only seven days—barely enough time to unpack his bags.

Also, Scripture provides the ages of all but two of Judah's kings, but no ages are given for the kings of Israel. Perhaps this is a subtle reminder of God's intimate care of David's line, which was preserved in the tribe of Judah. The youngest kings were Joash, who began his reign at the ripe old age of seven, and Josiah, who had a little more seniority at age eight. Several teens also took the throne: Uzziah, age sixteen; Manasseh, age twelve; and Jehoiachin, age eighteen.

Next, consider a sampling of intriguing scenes from the kings' lives. King Asa of Judah, as we'll see in chapter 3 of our study, followed the Lord so devotedly that he removed his own mother from her royal position because she worshiped idols (1 Kings 15:13).

Treacherous King Ahab, on the other hand, tried to escape notice in battle by using good King Jehoshaphat as a decoy. The Lord wasn't fooled, however, for "a certain man drew his bow at random" and killed Ahab despite his machinations (22:29–38).

Ahab's widow, the murderous Jezebel, was thrown from a window and killed; when her enemies went down to bury her, all they found were her skull, feet, and the palms of her hands—a fulfillment of Elijah's prophecy (2 Kings 9:30–37). Uzziah, a good king for most of his life, fell by his own pride, ending his reign as a leper (2 Chron. 26:16–21).

On the happier side, the righteousness of Judah's King Hezekiah provided the brightest light in the nation's history since David himself (2 Kings 18:1–6). Under Hezekiah's reign, the Levites cleansed the temple and Passover was celebrated—some from Israel

4

even joined them (2 Chron. 29–30). And God granted this king fifteen more years of life, hearing his prayer and healing him of a fatal illness (2 Kings 20:1–7).

His son and grandson, however, Manasseh and Amon, didn't follow the Lord but polluted the land with such idolatry as had never been known in Judah before (2 Kings 21). In fact, the writer of Kings records,

> Surely at the command of the Lord [war] came upon Judah, to remove them from His sight because of the sins of Manasseh, according to all that he had done, and also for the innocent blood which he shed, for he filled Jerusalem with innocent blood; and the Lord would not forgive. (24:3–4)

Only one more good king would reign in Judah: young Josiah, who would find the Book of the Law and institute one last era of reform (2 Kings 22–23). After him, Judah would spiral downward through four more idolatrous kings, finally hitting bottom with the Babylonian captivity.

It's hard to imagine idolatry taking such a hold among God's people, especially in the face of tenacious prophets who cut to the quick with the truth.

Elijah, Elisha, Amos, and Hosea prophesied primarily in the northern kingdom of Israel, but they proclaimed God's word to both Israel and Judah. In the southern kingdom of Judah, Obadiah, Joel, Micah, Isaiah, Nahum, Zephaniah, Jeremiah, and Habakkuk attempted to turn the Jews' hearts back to their God. And Jonah's divine message actually saved Israel's enemies in Assyria.

All of these prophets had an interesting job description: comfort the afflicted and afflict the comfortable. To the widow, the orphan, and those who truly sought the Lord, these men were like a breath of fresh air or a drink of cool water. But to wicked kings who had settled into the cozy cushions of sin, the prophets' voices grated on the nerves like fingernails on a blackboard. These holy spokesmen regularly put their lives on the line to deliver the message of Almighty God.

Crazy Days

It's hard to wrap all the events of this period into a package for overview. Generally speaking, though, we can summarize Kings and Chronicles into three themes.

5

The consequences and chaos brought by sin. The Hebrews showed us that peace, orderliness, and freedom will elude a society that persists in rebellion against God. Sin only breeds more sin, until the very fabric of a society begins to unravel.

The courage and the struggles of the prophets who spoke for God. Such people as Elijah and Jeremiah remind us that God uses ordinary people to accomplish extraordinary things. These men stood toe-to-toe with kings and declared God's word when that was the last thing the rulers wanted to hear. Yet the prophets were human. Elijah despaired of his life, and Jeremiah wept over the destruction of Jerusalem.

The faithfulness of God in preserving His nation. Most of the kings were bad. Some were good. A few, like Hezekiah and Josiah, were great. As hopeless as the state of God's people sometimes seemed, though, Kings and Chronicles should encourage us that God will never allow the wind of sin to snuff out His light in the world.

Where Was God in All This?

One who reads about this period of spiritual poverty might draw the conclusion that God lost control or relinquished His authority for a time. Or that He simply couldn't handle the situation. Or that He was absent when He was needed most.

On the contrary, He was there all along, as He is today. Sin doesn't drive God away. Sovereignty doesn't depend on circumstances; it determines them. And omnipresence and omniscience don't dissolve under pressure or diminish when God's people rebel against Him. God was there all right, in the midst of His people—urging leaders to hear and obey, speaking His word and will through the prophets, and fulfilling His own grim predictions about sin's consequences.

There's Gold in Them Thar Pages!

Well, we've just begun to dig. There's a lot more gold waiting to be discovered in Kings and Chronicles. Let's take one final look at what we've unearthed today.

First, we've learned that *sin still has its consequences.* God is infinitely gracious and patient with us. But He often allows sin to run its painful course so we'll learn how destructive it is. We shouldn't presume that, because God is merciful, He will always step in and rescue us from the consequences of our own choices. We do, after all, reap what we sow (Gal. 6:7).

Second, *righteousness always has its representatives*. The wickedness of Ahab couldn't snuff out Elijah's light. And who remembers the kings of Elisha's time as well as they do Elisha? In Judah's darkest days, godly kings, priests, and prophets all tried to lead the people back to God. So no matter how bleak things get, there will always be those who will stand like a mountain against the winds of evil.

Third, *God never forgets His promises*. God does whatever He says He will do—whether it's rescuing His people from ruin, sending them into captivity for their sin, or raising up a Messiah from their lineage. His Word and His ways are perfect, unfailing, and completely trustworthy.

So stake your claim right here in Kings and Chronicles. You won't come out empty-handed!

Living Insights

Israel wasn't divided just geographically. She was also divided spiritually. We could label one group the "go-alongs." These were the people with no moral rudder. They merely unfurled their spiritual sails and waited for them to swell with whatever wind was in vogue. If the majority worshiped idols, the go-alongs worshiped idols. If the prevailing attitude toward God was disobedience, they disobeyed. They would rather go along with the crowd than rock the boat by bringing God's desires into the discussion. They preferred pleasure over piety, comfort over holiness, self-rule over God's rule.

Then there were the "stand-alones." Their compass was the Word of God; and their rudder, their convictions. They didn't care whether they rocked the boat or not, as long as they followed God. They would rather die going in the right direction than live a day adrift in godlessness. They stood and spoke for God when it seemed that no one else would.

With which group do you most identify? The "go-alongs" or the "stand-alones"?

_____

_____

If you're a "stand-alone," what do you think has made you that way? Personality? Upbringing? Your personal study of Scripture?

_____

_____

_____

What would you like to gain from this study? How to help others develop strong convictions? How to communicate your beliefs more sensitively and empathetically? How to distinguish which issues are worth fighting for and which ones should be left alone?

_____

_____

_____

If you're a "go-along," to what do you attribute your membership in that group? Are you afraid of alienating others? Do you let others determine what you should believe instead of forging your own convictions from the Bible? Perhaps you're simply uncomfortable in situations that call for conflict.

_____

_____

_____

What would you like to gain from this study? A deeper understanding of who God is? A love for righteousness and a disdain for sin? A deeper commitment to God's Word? Perhaps something else?

_____

_____

_____

Now complete the study with these goals in mind. And ask the Holy Spirit to burn these lessons from Israel's history into your heart. Then, when history repeats itself, you can stand strong . . . and alone, if necessary.

Chapter 2

PRAISE GOD FROM WHOM ALL BLESSINGS FLOW

1 Chronicles 29:1–22

I'm so afraid. Give me the strength to die well."

The request, spoken heavenward, broke the dungeon's silence. The speaker was alone, except for several blades of silver-blue light that had sliced through the barred window and fanned across the cell floor. They stood almost ceremoniously, a silent tribute to a warrior who would soon be martyred.

The prisoner heard no reply, only the clanking of his chains. Yet he seemed to trust that God had listened. He uttered the prayer with the finality and conviction that had come to characterize his life. He knew the English would try to get him to beg for mercy— thus gaining a tacit admission of guilt—before executing him. But he didn't ask for a miraculous rescue. He asked only that in death he might champion freedom and defy tyranny as he had in life. His request was answered.

During his agonizing torture in London's town square, Scottish freedom fighter William Wallace never recanted or cried out for mercy. Instead, moments before the executioner's ax fell, he screamed one word: "Freedom!"

William Wallace, played by Mel Gibson in the Academy Award-winning film *Braveheart,* had long dreamed of a free Scotland. But he never got to live that dream—he was betrayed and turned over to his enemies. It would be nine years later, at the Battle of Bannockburn, that his followers would finally loose Scotland from England's grip.

Yet Wallace's realization that he would die before living his dream didn't dampen his passion for freedom or alter his convictions. With his last breath, he honored the country he loved and the men who followed him. He had served Scotland well.

Have you had any dreams or goals that you never got to live out? Plans that you had to put on hold? Harder yet, did you ever want to do something great, and God said, "Sorry, I've reserved that for someone else"?

We probably all have. And we've all probably responded with anger toward God or hate for the other person. Or decided that God was unfair. Or even allowed disappointment to weaken our character and convictions. Sometimes, though, we manage to stay focused on God, embracing His sovereignty and realizing that He uses whom He will for His glory.

It isn't easy to be spiritual when we have to let go of our dreams. We can find help, however, in the story of a king who wanted to do one great thing for God before he died, and God said no. His name was David.

A King's Dream

King David had it all. Wealth, power, respect, and, most importantly, a heart for God. The pomp of royalty couldn't suffocate his passion for the living God, as evidenced by his desire to build a dwelling place for the Lord.

> And it came about, when David dwelt in his house, that David said to Nathan the prophet, "Behold, I am dwelling in a house of cedar, but the ark of the covenant of the Lord is under curtains." (1 Chron. 17:1)

David had ushered the ark into Jerusalem amid great celebration (15:25–28). He had even danced before it, to the dismay of his wife (v. 29). Yet that wasn't enough. "Isn't God more powerful, more permanent than humankind?" David must have wondered. "He shouldn't be living in a tent; He deserves a house of His own."

What zeal. What eternal perspective. How could God turn down an offer like that? Look, though, at God's words to David through the prophet Nathan:

> "Go and tell David My servant, 'Thus says the Lord, "You shall not build a house for Me to dwell in."'" (17:4)

Ouch. Who will build it then?

> "'"And it shall come about when your days are fulfilled that you must go to be with your fathers, that I will set up one of your descendants after you, who shall be of your sons; and I will establish his kingdom.

He shall build for Me a house, and I will establish
his throne forever.""" (vv. 11–12)

David's son, Solomon, would be the temple's builder. God
wanted His temple built during a time of peace by a king of peace,
rather than a warrior (22:8–10).

How easy it would be to respond to such news, "That's not fair! I
thought of it; I should get to build it." Not David. Who was he, after
all, to argue with God's plan? Instead, David drew up the blueprints,
prepared materials for the construction, and encouraged Solomon
to see the project through to the glory of God (chaps. 22, 28).

An amazing response to disappointing news. But these actions
don't display David's heart nearly as much as his grateful prayer of
praise in 1 Chronicles 29.

The Context of David's Prayer

With the end of his life imminent, David assembled the leaders
of Israel to encourage them to follow Solomon and join him in
building this magnificent temple (vv. 1–9). The people responded
with overwhelming, spontaneous generosity. And a joyful David
turned to the Lord in worship. The king's prayer revolved around
three topics: Solomon's inexperience, God's provisions, and the
people's generosity.

Solomon's Inexperience

David wanted to pray for the success of his son Solomon, whose
young life lacked the experience to excel in a project of this magnitude.

> Then King David said to the entire assembly,
> "My son Solomon, whom alone God has chosen, is
> still young and inexperienced and the work is great;
> for the temple is not for man, but for the Lord God."
> (v. 1; see also 1 Kings 3:7)

In a sense, we're all like Solomon. God often gives us tasks that
make us feel inadequate, like a two-year-old trying to run a corpo-
ration. Yet He enables us to do the very things He requires. And
prayer puts us in touch with His power. Young Solomon needed
God's divine empowerment.

God's Provisions

David had gathered the raw materials—gold, silver, stones,

jewels, and wood (vv. 2–5)—and they were ready to be fashioned and fitted into a magnificent temple. What better time to acknowledge God's gracious provisions and dedicate them to His glory?

The People's Generosity

Israel's generosity also inspired David to pray. Just look at all they brought, above and beyond what David had already amassed.

> Then the rulers of the fathers' households, and the princes of the tribes of Israel, and the commanders of thousands and of hundreds, with the overseers over the king's work, offered willingly; and for the service for the house of God they gave 5,000 talents and 10,000 darics of gold, and 10,000 talents of silver, and 18,000 talents of brass, and 100,000 talents of iron. And whoever possessed precious stones gave them to the treasury of the house of the Lord, in care of Jehiel the Gershonite. Then the people rejoiced because they had offered so willingly, for they made their offering to the Lord with a whole heart, and King David also rejoiced greatly. (vv. 6–9)

Temple mount in Jerusalem. Most likely, Solomon's temple stood right where the modern-day Dome of the Rock (domed building) now stands. Though David was not permitted by God to build the temple, he undertook the enormous task of drawing up the blueprints and collecting the gold, silver, wood, and precious jewels for the furniture and articles of worship (1 Chron. 28:11–19; 29:1–5).

The Content of David's Prayer

With the prayer's foundation firmly in place, let's now look at the actual words David prayed and see how his eternal perspective allowed him to handle God's no.

Gratitude for Who God Is

For one thing, David had a grasp of God's greatness and His ownership of the universe.

> So David blessed the Lord in the sight of all the assembly; and David said, "Blessed art Thou, O Lord God of Israel our father, forever and ever. Thine, O Lord, is the greatness and the power and the glory and the victory and the majesty, indeed everything that is in the heavens and the earth; Thine is the dominion, O Lord, and Thou dost exalt Thyself as head over all. Both riches and honor come from Thee, and Thou dost rule over all, and in Thy hand is power and might; and it lies in Thy hand to make great, and to strengthen everyone. Now therefore, our God, we thank Thee, and praise Thy glorious name. But who am I and who are my people that we should be able to offer as generously as this? For all things come from Thee, and from Thy hand we have given Thee." (vv. 10–14)

Now that's perspective! When we focus on God, when we come to grips with His complete ownership of our lives and His infinite power and wisdom, we can put our dreams in His hands with complete confidence.

Acknowledgment of God's Provisions

In fact, David acknowledged that were it not for God's gracious blessings, Israel would have had nothing to use in the building of the temple.

> "For we are sojourners before Thee, and tenants, as all our fathers were; our days on the earth are like a shadow, and there is no hope. O Lord our God, all this abundance that we have provided to build Thee a house for Thy holy name, it is from Thy hand, and all is Thine. Since I know, O my God, that

13

Thou triest the heart and delightest in uprightness, I, in the integrity of my heart, have willingly offered all these things; so now with joy I have seen Thy people, who are present here, make their offerings willingly to Thee." (vv. 15–17)

Did you notice? David didn't get the praise. The people didn't get the praise. Because, by nature, praise is like a series of arrows that point upward and outward—always to God.

Petitions on Behalf of Those God Blesses

Next, David's praise turned to petition.

"O Lord, the God of Abraham, Isaac, and Israel, our fathers, preserve this forever in the intentions of the heart of Thy people, and direct their heart to Thee; and give to my son Solomon a perfect heart to keep Thy commandments, Thy testimonies, and Thy statutes, and to do them all, and to build the temple, for which I have made provision." (vv. 18–19)

The king after God's own heart prayed that the people, and especially his son Solomon, would keep their hearts fixed on God and follow His commandments.

Such intercession keeps us from pride. It's hard to envy others when you're praying for their success. "Since I won't be around to live my dream," said David, "let those who live it do so in God's strength and for His glory."

After David's display of heartfelt praise, how could the people keep from joining him in corporate worship (vv. 20–22)?

The Benefits of Praise

Who benefits from such times of praise and thanksgiving, and how?

First, *praise pleases God*. God loves it when we take the time to see His wonder and bless His name. Even certain offerings in the Old Testament were designated as praise offerings, reminding the Israelites to make room for gratitude in their lives (Lev. 19:23–25). The Psalms are packed with ways to extol God from our hearts for His character and works. And salvation itself inspires a new language of thankfulness and awe in those who receive God's unsearchable grace (Eph. 1:5–6).

Second, *praise blesses us.* Here's where we find help for broken dreams. Glorifying God takes our eyes off ourselves and brings Him into clear focus. It replaces anxiety with awe, worry with worship, our inability with His ability (see Ps. 8).

Third, *praise affects those around us.* As Solomon watched his father David in praise and intercessory prayer, he learned something of God's greatness. Paul and Silas, after being beaten and thrown in prison, sang hymns, and the other inmates heard of a hope that had long eluded them (Acts 16:25). As people see us adoring our heavenly Father, they learn something about His strength, His sufficiency, and His goodness.

We may not get to live out all our dreams. But we can be sure we fit into God's great plan somehow. After all, He saved us. He gave us gifts to use for His glory. And He promised never to leave us. What can we do then, except praise Him?

Living Insights

When life is at its lowest, praise gives us a higher perspective. It reminds us that God is still sovereign, that He still loves us, that He has never failed us, and that history is proceeding according to His plan. David could hand over to Solomon his dream of building the temple because he had God's vantage point.

The Puritans had that perspective too. Just read some of their prayers, and you'll learn anew what it means to give praise and honor to our majestic King. In fact, take some time right now to read the following prayer from the pen of a grateful Puritan. Don't rush; linger over the words. And let Him who prompted them draw you close to Himself.

> O LORD GOD, WHO INHABITEST ETERNITY,
> The heavens declare thy glory,
> The earth thy riches,
> The universe is thy temple;
> Thy presence fills immensity,
> Yet thou hast of thy pleasure created life, and
> communicated happiness;
> Thou hast made me what I am, and given me
> what I have;

In thee I live and move and have my being;
Thy providence has set the bounds of my
    habitation, and wisely administers all my
    affairs.
I thank thee for thy riches to me in Jesus,
    for the unclouded revelation of him in thy
    Word,
        where I behold his person, character, grace,
        glory, humiliation, sufferings, death, and
        resurrection;
Give me to feel a need of his continual
    saviourhood, and cry with Job, "I am vile,"
        with Peter, "I perish,"
        with the publican, "Be merciful to me, a
        sinner."
Subdue in me the love of sin,
Let me know the need of renovation as well as of
    forgiveness, in order to serve and enjoy thee
    for ever.
I come to thee in the all-prevailing name of Jesus,
        with nothing of my own to plead,
        no works, no worthiness, no promises.
I am often straying,
        often knowingly opposing thy authority,
        often abusing thy goodness;
Much of my guilt arises from my religious
    privileges,
        my low estimation of them,
        my failure to use them to my advantage,
But I am not careless of thy favour or regardless
    of thy glory;
Impress me deeply with a sense of thine
    omnipresence, that thou art about my path, my
    ways, my lying down, my end.[1]

The next time one of your dreams slips away, come back to this snowy peak of perspective. And let Him who is above all lift and refresh your soul.

---

1. "God the Source of All Good," in *The Valley of Vision: A Collection of Puritan Prayers and Devotions*, ed. Arthur Bennett (1975; reprint, Carlisle, Pa.: Banner of Truth Trust, 1995), p. 5.

Chapter 3

EROSION:
IT STARTS AT THE TOP

1 Kings 14; 2 Chronicles 10–12

W hat a tragedy. A multimillion-dollar house reduced to a heap of sticks in just a few seconds. Fire? Nope. Earthquake? Not this time. Hurricane? Guess again.

It's a mud slide.

Once a mud slide starts, there's no way to stop it. A relentless rain pummels the side of a hill, turning packed dirt into a downhill gush of grimy goo. And if your dream house is in the way, look out. Once the dirt around the foundation begins to wash away, there's nothing left to hold the house in place. All you can do is watch your home slide down the hill and crumble into a muddy, mangled mass of lumber.

Like a mud slide, Israel's spiritual slippage started at the top of the hill—with King Solomon. It gained momentum with his son Rehoboam, whose foolishness divided Israel into two nations. Then *crash*. Both Israel and Judah were taken into captivity as punishment for their shameless idolatry and brazen immorality.

Unlike a mud slide, however, spiritual erosion can be stopped —if we'll turn to the Lord and follow His Word.

Do you sometimes feel as though the solid ground beneath your spiritual house is starting to get a little slushy? Then let's look at the life of Rehoboam and his father's legacy for some lessons on how to stop—even prevent—spiritual erosion in our lives.

A Quick Glance at Rehoboam's Roots

As with all of us, Rehoboam's life was shaped by a variety of forces, the most powerful of which was his father.

His Father, Solomon

> Thus the time that Solomon reigned in Jerusalem over all Israel was forty years. And Solomon slept with his fathers and was buried in the city of his father David, and his son Rehoboam reigned in his place. (1 Kings 11:42–43)

Solomon reigned for forty years. And if we compare chronologies, we see that Rehoboam assumed the throne when he was forty-one years old (1 Kings 14:21). That means Solomon began his rule when Rehoboam was a year old. So Rehoboam grew up in the splendid surroundings of royalty.

"What an enviable heritage!" one might say. And it was in many respects. Solomon was the talk of his day. He was brilliant, wise, creative, and industrious. Free from war and basking in the warm light of peace, Solomon undertook numerous building projects, including the construction of the Lord's temple. Wealth and wisdom adorned his kingdom as the stars adorn the heavens. He was the envy of every king and queen. And Rehoboam was right there in the middle of it all. He saw his father rise to prominence . . . and he saw him slide into immorality. G. Frederick Owen provides a chilling summary of Solomon's decline. For probably the first half of his reign,

> wisdom, loyalty, faithfulness and efficiency charac-
> terized the attitudes and acts of David's brilliant
> son. . . . Then, as if he had attained the mastery
> of man and God, he turned from following the Lord,
> and selfishly seizing the reins of wrong, drove to the
> misty flats of licentiousness, pride and paganism.
> Maddened with the love of show, Solomon swung
> into a feverish career of wastefulness, impropriety,
> and oppression. Not satisfied with the necessary
> buildings and legitimate progress of his past years,
> he over-burdened his people with taxation [and es-
> tablished forced labor]. . . . All Solomon's drink-
> ing vessels were of gold, and those of his house were
> of pure gold. The shields of his mighty men were
> made of beaten gold, and his great throne was made
> of ivory and overlaid with the finest gold. Silver in
> Jerusalem became as common as stones.
>
> Solomon literally built himself a *paradise of
> pleasure*. . . .
>
> . . . His love for *many* women caused him to
> marry and pamper numerous foreign, heathen wives,
> who not only robbed him of his excellency of char-
> acter, humility of spirit, and efficiency in state affairs,
> but dominated him and turned his heart to seek
> "after other gods." Just across the "king's vale" on a

hill overlooking the village of Siloam, strange edifices arose before the eyes of the awe-stricken Hebrews. Solomon was building temples for the strange gods he and his strange wives were serving.[1]

Solomon's Flawed Philosophy

Among other things, Rehoboam inherited from his father a faulty philosophy of leadership: "The king has divine rights." In other words, he does whatever he wants—regardless of who suffers or whether his actions honor God.

Such a philosophy as Solomon's has been the downfall of many a leader. Those who view themselves as infallible, exclusive, and accountable to no one are destined to fall. Such people fail to see themselves as stewards whom God has granted the privilege and responsibility of leading. Instead of serving the people, they demand service from them; they lord their leadership over those they should be helping. These leaders, sooner or later, must come to terms with a God who shares His glory with no one.

Those in positions of leadership—pastors, teachers, heads of companies, parents, etc.—beware. Whether you're conscious of it or not, you're passing on a philosophy of living to those under your authority.

Now let's see just how Rehoboam's life continued the spiritual slide started by his father, Solomon.

A Closer Look at Rehoboam's Reign

Scripture reveals several reasons why Rehoboam contributed to the spiritual erosion of Israel.

Listened to Unwise Counsel

First, *he listened to the unwise counsel of his contemporaries instead of heeding the wisdom of the elders.* Rehoboam showed his pride when some of his people approached him about the high taxes they had to pay.

> Then Rehoboam went to Shechem, for all Israel had come to Shechem to make him king. Now it came about when Jeroboam the son of Nebat heard

---

1. G. Frederick Owen, *Abraham to the Middle-East Crisis,* 4th ed. (Grand Rapids, Mich.: William B. Eerdmans Publishing Co., 1957), pp. 56–57. If you want to read further about Solomon, see 1 Kings 2–11 and 2 Chronicles 1–9.

of it, that he was living in Egypt (for he was yet in Egypt, where he had fled from the presence of King Solomon). Then they sent and called him, and Jeroboam and all the assembly of Israel came and spoke to Rehoboam, saying, "Your father made our yoke hard; therefore lighten the hard service of your father and his heavy yoke which he put on us, and we will serve you." (1 Kings 12:1–4)

Notice with whom Rehoboam consulted first: "the elders who had served his father Solomon" (v. 6). These men knew what harsh rule and the pursuit of materialism could do—they had watched Solomon do the very same thing. And so they counseled Rehoboam,

"If you will be a servant to this people today, will serve them, grant them their petition, and speak good words to them, then they will be your servants forever." (v. 7)

In other words, "Lighten up, Rehoboam. Stop looking at these people as your personal income-producers. Be a servant to them. Help them, and they'll repay you with loyalty."

But Rehoboam ignored their counsel. Instead, he followed the advice of the "young men" (vv. 10–15), who urged him to turn the screws even tighter.

Leaders, choose your advisers wisely. Our only infallible counselor, of course, is God, particularly as He speaks through His Word. But we should also listen to those around us—especially those who have walked closely with God over a period of time and whose hearts and minds harbor the lessons of experience. Be wary of those who encourage you to take all you can at any cost.

Followed Parents' Weak Example

A second way Rehoboam kept the spiritual mud slide moving is that *he followed his parents' weak example at home rather than the timeless truths of Scripture.* Rehoboam's mother was not a devout Israelite but an idol-worshiping Ammonitess (see 2 Chron. 12:13). How could a worshiper of false gods possibly teach her son about following the true God? She couldn't, but Solomon could have.

Solomon addresses his teaching to "My son" so often in his book of Proverbs that one can't help but wonder if he were writing to Rehoboam. Unfortunately, it appears that Solomon's later actions spoke louder than his earlier words. Rehoboam didn't thirst after God the way Proverbs admonishes us to; rather, he soaked up the bad habits of his father.

Solomon oppressed the people; so did Rehoboam. Solomon was a polygamist; so was Rehoboam (see 2 Chron. 11:18–21). Both had concubines, both turned away from the Lord, and both allowed the worship of idols to flourish under their reigns (see 1 Kings 14:21–24). When we ignore God's Word, we fall prey to whatever influences happen to be surrounding us at the time.

A word of caution here for those whose parents neglected the spiritual life at home. A child with godless parents doesn't *have* to become godless. The fingers of God's grace can pluck a soul out of any environment, no matter how hopeless it may seem. And each of us is responsible to God for our own actions, regardless of how we were raised. So let's be aware of and learn from our parents' weaknesses, but let's not use them as an excuse for our own disobedience.

As for those who are still raising children, don't use the vast scope of God's grace as an excuse to neglect the spiritual development of your family. He has, after all, set up the family as the primary field for the sowing of His Word (Deut. 6:1–9). For parents and children alike, Rehoboam's life teaches one simple truth with crystal clarity: Follow the Lord and obey His Word.

Refused to Seek the Lord

Third, *Rehoboam simply refused to seek the Lord.* Although Rehoboam's life wasn't all bad—he did humble himself before the Lord when Egypt invaded Jerusalem (2 Chron. 12:1–12)—it was characterized as rebellious against God.

> And he did evil because he did not set his heart to seek the Lord. (v. 14)

Rehoboam's personal rebellion didn't affect just him and his family; it fostered national rebellion. Judah lived in a constant state of civil war with Israel. And because of their idolatry, the Jews, God's chosen people, drifted from their loving Father and His favor. In the final analysis, Rehoboam is exposed as a weak-willed monarch who wore the garb of royalty but lived a hollow, tragic life. He's one of many kings who contributed to the downhill slide of God's people.

Rehoboam's foolishness not only divided the kingdom politically, it contributed to idolatry. Here at Dan, Rehoboam's rival, Jeroboam, built this high place to prevent the people from worshiping at the temple in Jerusalem (1 Kings 12:26–30).

A Sobering Response to Rehoboam's Wrongs

What can we learn from Rehoboam's participation in the erosion of Judah? Two final thoughts.

One, *any life can erode*. No one—no individual, no nation, no family, no church—is immune. We must all take precautions against succumbing to the influences that cause us to slip and slide away from God.

Second, *guard your heart*. When Solomon was still following God, he wrote:

> Watch over your heart with all diligence,
> For from it flow the springs of life. (Prov. 4:23)

Whatever seeps into our hearts flows out through our lives. So be careful about what you watch, where you spend your time, and what you think. Consult God about your decisions. Admit it when you're wrong. And develop a lifestyle of spiritual diligence—studying God's Word, thinking and living biblically. You only have to do one thing to cause erosion . . . nothing.

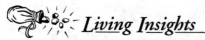 *Living Insights*

Do you see any signs of spiritual erosion in your life? What are they? A diminished interest in studying or reading the Bible? Rationalizing sin? An unhealthy attachment to material things? Have you stopped consulting with God on major decisions? Are you being influenced by those who couldn't care less about God? What other signs do you see?

_____

_____

_____

_____

_____

Make a list of activities that you know would help stop the slide. For example, developing a regular Bible study time or talking with a Christian friend or pastor about your struggle. Or making yourself accountable to someone for stopping a habitual sin. Write down whatever comes to mind.

_____   _____

_____   _____

_____   _____

_____   _____

Now pick one, and work it into your life this week. When it becomes a habit, work in another one. Stay with it. And you'll be climbing again instead of sliding.

_____

_____

_____

_____

_____

Chapter 4

THE BENEFITS OF GODLY, GUTSY COUNSEL

2 Chronicles 15

You never know how someone's going to respond to the truth.

A wife's question, "Do you like my new hairdo?" can create a dilemma for her husband, if he preferred the old coiffure. For example, should he lie and say he loves it, knowing the time and money she spent and sensing how good the change makes her feel? Should he wax diplomatic with "Honey, if you like it, I like it"? Should he venture boldly into vagueness: "Wow, honey, that's really—different"? Or should he tell the truth and risk bursting her bubble . . . and sleeping on the couch for the next couple of days?

Telling the truth can be dangerous! Especially if truth is the last thing the person on the receiving end wants to hear. Just ask the Old Testament prophets, who championed the truth, regardless of the consequences. They regularly jabbed the sharp point of God's truth into the inflated immorality of Israel and Judah. Often, their righteous confrontation angered kings and cost the prophets their lives. Sometimes, though, kings listened and obeyed, and whole nations turned to God.

We don't have the Old Testament prophets with us today. But we still have God's authoritative revelation in the form of Scripture. And with it, we're to encourage, counsel, even reprove one another. Does the fear of rejection, making someone mad, or potential persecution prevent you from laying out the truth in plain view? Or do you uphold truth without worrying about results? Or maybe your approach is *too* strong, and you need to learn how to "speak the truth in love," seasoning your convictions with humility, tact, and empathy.

On the flip side, how do you *respond* to truth? With openness, obedience, teachability, and confession? Or with resentment and stubbornness, rationalizing your behavior when it conflicts with God's revealed will?

Wherever you encounter God's Word—the worship service, counseling office, home, discipleship group—this lesson offers help for delivering the truth with conviction, clarity, and compassion and receiving it with reverence and humility. Our classroom is the fifteenth chapter of 2 Chronicles. Our instructors? A prophet named Azariah and a king named Asa.

God's Word through a Prophet

> Now the Spirit of God came on Azariah the son of Oded. (2 Chron. 15:1)

Azariah. The name means "helped by Jehovah."[1] An appropriate name for a prophet, who must not only communicate the words of God faithfully but trust Him to protect and provide—regardless of the listeners' response. More than twenty men in Scripture bear that name,[2] but the son of Oded appears only here in 2 Chronicles 15. His counsel, comprising a mere six verses, flashes across the Scripture like a shooting star. Yet he burns a message into the heart of a king, and a nation turns its wandering eyes back to the Lord.

The Setting

To appreciate Azariah's encounter with Asa, let's set the scene with a little background information.

Asa was the third king of Judah, the southern kingdom. Until Asa, Judah had been ruled by kings who rejected God. Rehoboam forsook the law of the Lord (2 Chron. 12:1), and his son Abijah followed in his steps (1 Kings 14:31–15:3). But Abijah's son, Asa, though not perfect, was Judah's first good king. He "did what was right in the sight of the Lord, like David his father" (1 Kings 15:11; see also 2 Chron. 14:2).

As an expression of his dependence on the Lord, Asa turned to Him for help in fighting the Ethiopians (2 Chron. 14:8–11); and God granted him victory over Zerah's massive army (vv. 12–15).

The Counsel

When do we tend to stop seeking God? When we convince ourselves that our own power is enough, that we can handle life without Him. Who knows, maybe Asa, with the adrenaline of victory still pulsing through his veins, was starting to think this

---

1. Merrill F. Unger, *Unger's Bible Dictionary* (Chicago, Ill.: Moody Press, 1966), p. 110.

2. Unger, *Unger's Bible Dictionary*, pp. 110–11.

way. So God, in His perfect timing, sent Azariah to remind the king to keep his eyes on Him.

> And he went out to meet Asa and said to him, "Listen to me, Asa, and all Judah and Benjamin: the Lord is with you when you are with Him. And if you seek Him, He will let you find Him; but if you forsake Him, He will forsake you." (2 Chron. 15:2)

That sounds a lot like the message God gave to Solomon (see 2 Chron. 7:17–22). Knowing the propensity of His people to sin, God continually had to remind the Jews, as He has to remind us, that rejection of Him and dependence on our own resources eventually brings destruction.

So let's take a closer look at Azariah's words. They have a lot to teach us about pursuing godliness and counseling others to do the same.

Notice, first of all, how *Azariah spoke with confidence and assurance.* Moved by the Spirit of God, Azariah went directly to Asa; he didn't wait for an invitation. And he got right to the point. No ambiguity here; no beating around the bush. He simply carried out the Lord's command, delivering His words with confidence—not in himself, but in the God who knows and controls all things.

Second, Azariah *did not hesitate to bring a strong warning.* "If you want closeness with God," the prophet counseled, "seek Him; if you want distance from God, forsake Him." As a pattern, the kings of both Israel and Judah sought God as a last resort, turning to Him only after being plundered by a pagan nation or tasting God's judgment.[3]

So Azariah reminded this king that God is willing to be found, and He blesses those who seek Him. "But if you desert God, Asa, then He will desert you." A strong warning. But when the spiritual health of an individual—or a nation—is at stake, such candor is not only appropriate, it is necessary.

Third, we learn from Azariah's counsel that *he understood God's hand in history.* His next words were a poignant reminder for Asa.

> "And for many days Israel was without the true God and without a teaching priest and without law. But

---

3. Even Asa, though characterized as a good king, would later turned to the king of Aram rather than God for help against an attack from Israel (2 Chron. 16:1–3). And this was *after* he had already witnessed God's deliverance from the Ethiopians.

in their distress they turned to the Lord God of Israel, and they sought Him, and He let them find Him. And in those times there was no peace to him who went out or to him who came in, for many disturbances afflicted all the inhabitants of the lands. And nation was crushed by nation, and city by city, for God troubled them with every kind of distress." (2 Chron. 15:3–6)

Why would Azariah recap all this dark history? To keep Asa from repeating it.

One of Israel's darkest times was the era recorded in Judges. The writer of that book describes the repeating cycle of God's people forsaking the Lord, the Lord letting other nations oppress His people, their crying out for deliverance, and God's rescue through one of His judges. The essence of those terrible times is captured in the echoing refrain: "In those days there was no king in Israel; everyone did what was right in his own eyes" (Judg. 17:6; 21:25).

Azariah would not have Asa drag the nation through that again. And God would not have us live that way either. That's why we need to study how He has worked in the past and learn from the lives of those who have embraced Him, denied Him, lived for Him, and died for Him.

Finally, *Azariah gave the king hope and reassurance.*

"But you, be strong and do not lose courage, for there is reward for your work." (v. 7)

What an encouragement these words must have been to Asa. Though Israel's past was stained with national disobedience, the king was free to pursue a righteous course. "God is still involved," comforted the prophet. "Take courage, for He still recognizes and rewards those who do good." The prophet's words harmonize with the book of Hebrews.

For God is not unjust so as to forget your work and the love which you have shown toward His name, in having ministered and in still ministering to the saints. (Heb. 6:10)

Paul echoed the same thoughts in Galatians.

And let us not lose heart in doing good, for in due time we shall reap if we do not grow weary. So then, while we have opportunity, let us do good to all men, and especially to those who are of the household of the faith. (Gal. 6:9–10)

It's never too late to start walking with God, to start living a life that pleases Him. Regardless of our history—personal or national—God stands ready to employ us in His work and bless us for our efforts.

God's Work in a King

And that's the last we hear of Azariah the prophet. But his words shook Asa's soul like a wind from heaven, stirring him to instigate righteous reform.

Asa's Response

> Now when Asa heard these words and the prophecy which Azariah the son of Oded the prophet spoke, he took courage and removed the abominable idols from all the land of Judah and Benjamin and from the cities which he had captured in the hill country of Ephraim. He then restored the altar of the Lord which was in front of the porch of the Lord. (2 Chron. 15:8)

Idol worship started with Solomon and continued through the next two reigns (Rehoboam and Abijah). Asa had the courage and the heart for God to break the cycle. So he went on an idol-smashing spree across the country and reintroduced the worship of the Lord.

Now watch what happened.

> And he gathered all Judah and Benjamin and those from Ephraim, Manasseh, and Simeon who resided with them, for many defected to him from Israel when they saw that the Lord his God was with him. (v. 9)

Amazing, isn't it? When the unmistakable fragrance of God emanates from one individual's life, people notice. They're either terrified by God's presence or they flock to it, wide-eyed with fascination. Even some in the northern kingdom, Israel, unfulfilled by a religion as lifeless as the idols they worshiped, defected to Judah to participate in this work of God.

The spiritual hole left by uprooted idols was quickly filled with the worship of the true God (vv. 10–11). Even more exciting, the people renewed their commitment to seek the Lord (vv. 12–15). What a scene! As the bleating of sheep and the lowing of cattle ascended from Jerusalem, and as the people raised their hands and voices in praise, the words of Azariah the prophet must have echoed inside Asa's head: "If you seek Him, He will let you find Him." Asa sought Him, all right; so did the people. And the Lord answered with revival.

Asa validated his renewed commitment to the Lord by removing his own mother, Maacah, from her position as queen mother.[4] Why?

> Because she had made a horrid image as an Asherah, and Asa cut down her horrid image, crushed it and burned it at the brook Kidron. (v. 16b)

The words of Jesus come to mind here.

> "Do not think that I came to bring peace on the earth; I did not come to bring peace, but a sword. For I came to set a man against his father, and a daughter against her mother, and a daughter-in-law against her mother-in-law; and a man's enemies will be the members of his household. He who loves father or mother more than Me is not worthy of Me; and he who loves son or daughter more than Me is not worthy of Me." (Matt. 10:34–37)

We're to honor our parents. But if our relationship with them takes a higher priority than our relationship with Christ, we're out of focus spiritually. Asa was willing to endanger his ties with his own mother in order to restore righteousness to his nation.

Coupled with this rejuvenation, though, is the reality of man's tendency to wander. Though Asa walked with God, "the high places were not removed from Israel" (2 Chron. 15:17a). "High places" were sites of pagan altars. Some of them remained. And like an evil weed that was only clipped but not pulled out by the roots, idolatry eventually grew again in the land as it spread from Israel to Judah.

---

4. "(The Hebrew *em* can mean either 'mother,' NASB, or 'grandmother,' NIV.) As 'queen mother' she may have been Asa's mother; if so it is coincidental that his grandmother was also named Maacah (cf. 11:20)." Eugene H. Merrill, "2 Chronicles," in *The Bible Knowledge Commentary*, Old Testament edition, ed. John F. Walvoord and Roy B. Zuck (Wheaton, Ill.: Scripture Press Publications, Victor Books, 1985), p. 632.

"Nevertheless," the chronicler adds, "Asa's heart was blameless all his days" (v. 17b). As an example of that, we are told that he restocked the temple with riches (v. 18) to replace what had been plundered by Shishak, the Egyptian king who invaded Judah during Rehoboam's reign.

The Results of Obedience

For the next twenty years, God let peace rest on Judah, proof that obedience brings blessing (v. 19; see also v. 15b). Obeying God sometimes seems like the hardest road to take. But in the long run, it's the only lifestyle that brings real peace and genuine joy.

God's Word in Counseling

Our delivery of God's Word won't mirror Azariah's, since we are not prophets with direct revelation from God. And unlike king Asa, our ministry probably doesn't include roaming the countryside in search of idols to smash. But the Word of God is still our spiritual authority. And we can learn a lot from these two men about how to counsel others from the Word and encourage them to godliness. Here are a few points to remember.

First, *if you are the one giving counsel, think and talk the truth.* Azariah didn't let Asa's potential response muffle the Word of God. He laid the truth out there, because God directed him to do it. As painfully revealing as the truth can be, we do no one a favor by withholding it. Proverbs says,

> A truthful witness saves lives,
> But he who speaks lies is treacherous.
> (Prov. 14:25)

Second, *if you are the one receiving counsel, hear and heed what is said.* Asa could have walked away from Azariah, but he didn't. He listened, he acted on what he heard, and God honored his obedience. Attentiveness to godly counsel brings wisdom, as Solomon said:

> Listen to counsel and accept discipline,
> That you may be wise the rest of your days.
> Many are the plans in a man's heart,
> But the counsel of the Lord, it will stand.
> (Prov. 19:20–21)

Third, *if you hope to change, start strong and go the distance.* Digging into the deep layers of your life is an arduous journey. It takes time, commitment, and concentration. It may strain relationships that function in unbiblical, unhealthy ways. And you'll always run the risk of being misunderstood by those who don't want to change. But our persistence keeps us increasingly pliable to God's truth. God doesn't give up on us, so let's not give up on ourselves. Another spokesman for God said,

> Blessed is a man who perseveres under trial; for once he has been approved, he will receive the crown of life, which the Lord has promised to those who love Him. (James 1:12)

Living Insights

> And [Asa] also removed Maacah, the mother of King Asa, from the position of queen mother, because she had made a horrid image as an Asherah, and Asa cut down her horrid image, crushed it and burned it at the brook Kidron. (2 Chron. 15:16)

With fresh courage from God's message in his heart, Asa destroyed the false gods that were leading his people astray and restored the altar of the only true and living God. Then he assembled God's people to make sacrifices and, more importantly, to make a covenant to seek the Lord with "all their heart and soul." This was followed by an oath, where everyone pledged to seek God earnestly, and God "let them find Him." And Judah had peace.

But it wasn't the easiest peace for Asa. To attain it, he had to honestly address and then deal with the corruption in the royal family. *His* royal family. In the end, he had to bring to an end the godless, destructive influence of his own mother.

Now, not too many of us in America have to deal with idolatry in our families. Many of us, though, do have to come to terms with the sometimes hurtful influence of our families—those words and actions, past and present, that keep us from fully embracing our heavenly Father and His gift of life.

Is this something you struggle with? Perhaps this issue has surfaced in a counseling setting, in confrontation with your parents,

31

or in your personal prayer or Bible study time. Regardless of how it surfaced, we can still learn a lot about how to deal with it from Asa's courageous example.

If you were to sum up your family's legacy to you in one or two words, what words would you choose?

_____

_____

How do you see your family's influence working itself out in your life today? Are there feelings, perspectives, and patterns of dealing with life that trip you up more than help you along? Try to pinpoint a few.

_____

_____

_____

_____

How frankly are you addressing these hindrances? Are you committed to growing in Christ through this, following the One "who is at work in you, both to will and to work for His good pleasure" (Phil. 2:13)?

_____

_____

Having to unlearn one way of life and learn another, healthier way is no easy task. It really is arduous and often painful—but it is always worth it. So if you're in the thick of the struggle, don't give up. See it through. The Christian life is a journey, not a quick fix, and maturity doesn't come in an instant formula (see Rom. 7; 1 Cor. 9:24–27; Heb. 12:1; James 1:4).

He who created the universe with a mere spoken word is re-creating all of us through His Word and Spirit. And if He never gives up, why should we?

Chapter 5

IT ALL STARTS WITH THE HEART

2 Chronicles 15–16

When we first observed King Asa and the prophet Azariah in 2 Chronicles 15, we explored the human side of their story. We listened carefully to Azariah as he delivered God's message, looked back at his historical perspective, and felt the encouragement with which he infused the king's spirit. Then we watched how Asa's heart—aflame with God's righteousness—ignited a kingdom with revival.

As usual with God's Word, we uncovered some rich lessons. However, as important as learning from godly activity is, we need to be careful that we don't overlook God Himself in the process. How easy it is for us preoccupied people to miss Him—even though He is ever present, ever at work, and ever trying to communicate with us.

What is it that He's saying? What's the nature of the relationship He seeks with us? What does He want, and why? Let's revisit Asa's encounter with Azariah, taking some tours into other key Scriptures along the way, to find some answers.

What God Wants

Every love relationship consists of giving and taking, and our relationship with God is no different. What should we give Him in response to all He extends to us—His grace, love, power, and holiness? At least three general responses come to mind, with one specific response undergirding them all.

Generally

First, God wants our *obedience*. Not because He's some suffocating, dominating tyrant who gains His security by demanding control. That's humanity's fallen distortion. Rather, God, as the Author of all life, gives us precepts and principles that lead to blessing and our eternal well-being. That's what the Ten Commandments are all about (see Exod. 20:1–17), and that's what the psalmist made clear:

Thou wilt make known to me the path of life;
In Thy presence is fulness of joy;
In Thy right hand there are pleasures forever.
(Ps. 16:11)

Next, God desires our *praise*. God has no need to have His ego stroked. We, however, have a great need to see beyond ourselves and learn to worship. We can all take a lesson from David:

> So David blessed the Lord in the sight of all the assembly; and David said, "Blessed art Thou, O Lord God of Israel our father, forever and ever. Thine, O Lord, is the greatness and the power and the glory and the victory and the majesty, indeed everything that is in the heavens and the earth; Thine is the dominion, O Lord, and Thou dost exalt Thyself as head over all. Both riches and honor come from Thee, and Thou dost rule over all, and in Thy hand is power and might; and it lies in Thy hand to make great, and to strengthen everyone. Now therefore, our God, we thank Thee, and praise Thy glorious name." (1 Chron. 29:10–13; see also Heb. 13:15)

Third, God desires *right living* from us, a sensitivity to both one another and to Him. Micah makes this simple truth clear.

> He has told you, O man, what is good;
> And what does the Lord require of you
> But to do justice, to love kindness,
> And to walk humbly with your God?
> (Mic. 6:8; see also James 1:26–27; 1 John 4:20–21)

Specifically

All three of these general responses are the outworking of something deeper: our hearts. And God wants our hearts more than anything.

> "Hear, O Israel! The Lord is our God, the Lord is one! And you shall love the Lord your God with all your heart and with all your soul and with all your might. And these words, which I am commanding you today, shall be on your heart." (Deut. 6:4–6)

Why does God want our heart's deepest, most faithful love?

34

Because He knows that if you capture a person's heart, the rest of his or her life will follow. As Solomon said,

> Watch over your heart with all diligence,
> For from it flow the springs of life. (Prov. 4:23)

The heart is the private place where we make our decisions, entertain our deepest thoughts and most determined purposes. In other words, it all starts in the heart. Words and actions—both right and wrong, kind and cruel, strong and weak, courageous and cowardly. Just ask Joshua and Caleb.

They, along with ten others, had been sent by Moses to spy out the Promised Land. When they returned to the Israelites, the ten infected the whole camp with their intimidation at the size of the inhabitants and the fortification of their cities. And the people grumbled against God. Joshua and Caleb alone stood firm in God's power and promise (Num. 14). Notice what God said about these two men:

> "'None of the men who came up from Egypt, from twenty years old and upward, shall see the land which I swore to Abraham, to Isaac and to Jacob; for they did not follow Me fully, except Caleb the son of Jephunneh the Kenizzite and Joshua the son of Nun, for they have followed the Lord fully.'" (32:11–12)

They followed God *fully.* In the NIV, the word is "wholeheartedly." Totally, completely, thoroughly—that's the idea.[1] God wants our whole hearts and ultimately our whole lives (see Prov. 3:5–6).

Why God Wants Our Hearts

Does God collect hearts for sheer sport? To hang on His wall like trophies? No way. God can never be motivated by selfishness, greed, or pride; His holiness prevents it. So why does He desire our hearts? Let's return to Asa's encounter with Azariah in 2 Chronicles 15, where we find at least three reasons.

---

1. To "follow fully" is a single, descriptive word in Hebrew. Its root means "to be full" or "to fill," and its varied nuances can be seen in Genesis 6:13; Joshua 3:15; and 1 Kings 8:11.

To Reveal Himself to Us

Remember Azariah's historical account of a nation whose heart had drifted from God (2 Chron. 15:3–6)? He was probably referring to the period of the judges, when the nation of Israel kept churning through a cycle of disobedience, repentance, restoration. The less of their hearts they gave to God, the further they drifted from Him. There was no teaching of the Word (v. 3), no peace, and constant trouble (vv. 5–6). So Azariah warned Asa, "Don't you make the same mistake; seek God, and He'll let you find Him."

In other words, *God wants our hearts so He can reveal to us all that He is.* And "all" means His presence, His power, His plans, His purposes, and His promises.

You see, God isn't playing games with us. He's not trying to keep us guessing about His will. He wants to be found. But He only reveals Himself to those who honestly seek Him. The more of your heart you give to God, the more of His presence you'll experience.

To Instill Courageous Vision

Second, *God wants our hearts so we can have the courage to do visionary things.* Azariah completed his message to Asa with these words: "But you, be strong and do not lose courage, for there is reward for your work" (v. 7).

And Asa did take courage, so much so that he removed the idols from the land and restored the Lord's altar at His temple (v. 8). He had gained a vision for God's righteousness to be returned to Judah, and he found strength to pursue that vision, not because he was a strong man, but because his heart belonged to God. When God has our hearts, they beat in rhythm with His. We want what He wants. We see things from His perspective. And we fear Him more than we fear people.

To Give Us Rest

Finally, *God wants our hearts so He might give us rest on every side.* Asa's reform spread to the people of Judah, and they committed to following the Lord with their whole heart too (vv. 14–15). In response, God "let them find Him. So the Lord gave them rest on every side" (v. 15).

What does it mean to have "rest on every side"? According to the *Theological Wordbook of the Old Testament*, the Hebrew idea of rest signifies not only the absence of movement but being settled in a particular place . . . with over-tones of finality, or . . . of victory, salvation, etc.

Basically the root . . . relates to the absence of spatial activity and presence of security, as seen, e.g. in the ark which "rested" on Mount Ararat.[2]

That's what happens when we follow God with our whole hearts. He gives us rest—a sense of security. It's the absence of restlessness, a state of being settled in Him.

Haven't you seen this trait in godly individuals? They don't seem to get frazzled, no matter what life throws at them. Their walk doesn't waver; their faith remains strong and steady. That's because they know God well enough to rest in Him.

What God Does

We've seen that God wants our hearts and that He has good reasons for it. So what does He do to acquire them? Does He lounge around heaven, waiting for us to get His attention? Not according to 2 Chronicles 16:9a:

> "For the eyes of the Lord move to and fro throughout the earth that He may strongly support those whose heart is completely His."

These words came from Hanani the seer (v. 7). He was casti-gating Asa—yes, the same Asa who was blessed in chapter 15 — for trusting in the king of Aram instead of the Lord to deliver him from an attack by the northern kingdom. Unfortunately, not seeking help from God was a pattern in Asa's later life. Even when he contracted a terminal illness, he sought the help of physicians and not the Lord (v. 12).

Yet, as Hanani affirms, God is involved! What a rebuttal to the theory that God plays hard to get—toying with us, staying just out of our reach when we need Him the most. No, His all-seeing eyes rove the earth, mindful and active on behalf of "those whose heart is completely His."

---

2. R. Laird Harris, Gleason L. Archer, Jr., and Bruce K. Waltke, eds., *Theological Wordbook of the Old Testament* (Chicago, Ill.: Moody Press, 1980), vol. 2, p. 562.

This is a portion of the wall at Mizpah built by Asa with stones he brought from Ramah (1 Kings 15:22; 2 Chron. 16:6). This was the result of his alliance with the King of Aram, which God called "foolish" (2 Chron. 16:9).

The word *completely* is a richly textured word in Hebrew. The root, *shalem*, and its related words weave together a tapestry of wholeness, harmony, and unimpaired relationships with "the status of being at peace with God."[3]

Peace with God—that's what is meant by a heart that is completely His. It means we are in harmony with the Lord; our relationship with Him is unimpaired; our will is in step with His. In New Testament language, we are reconciled with Him (see Rom. 5:10–11; 2 Cor. 5:18–21; Eph. 2:13–22; Col. 1:19–23).

Why God Does It

Why does God look for hearts that are at peace with Him? Let's look once more at 2 Chronicles 16:9.

> "For the eyes of the Lord move to and fro throughout
> the earth *that He may strongly support* those whose
> heart is completely His." (emphasis added)

Imagine that. The Creator of the universe, the Most High God, standing ready to help His people. God didn't craft the world and

---

3. Harris, Archer, and Waltke, *Theological Wordbook of the Old Testament*, pp. 931, 932.

then spin it into space to take care of itself. He is actively, powerfully involved with His people. And He is intimately, tenderly nurturing too (see Isa. 40:11; Ezek. 34:11–16). What tremendous truth!

What We Need to Do

The whole of Scripture teaches about a God who not only made the world but participates in it, upholds it, directs it. Such a God deserves our hearts, our hands, our lives. He deserves not our leftovers but the very best we can give. As Paul urged,

> Whatever you do in word or deed, do all in the name of the Lord Jesus, giving thanks through Him to God the Father. (Col. 3:17)

Living Insights

You may be reading this and thinking, "My heart is in no shape to give to God; that's the last thing I want to turn over to Him. It's unclean—filled with false motives, anxiety, anger, fear, and insecurity." Perhaps the words of Jeremiah come to mind:

> "The heart is more deceitful than all else
> And is desperately sick;
> Who can understand it?" (Jer. 17:9)

Well, don't despair; there's good news. God not only searches our hearts, He changes our hearts. He molds them and shapes them until they resemble His own and beat with the same eternal rhythm. Ezekiel put it this way:

> "'"I will give you a new heart and put a new spirit within you; and I will remove the heart of stone from your flesh and give you a heart of flesh. And I will put My Spirit within you and cause you to walk in My statutes, and you will be careful to observe My ordinances. And you will live in the land that I gave to your forefathers; so you will be My people, and I will be your God."'" (Ezek. 36:26–28)

David, heavy with the sin of adultery with Bathsheba, sought the cleansing forgiveness of God when he prayed,

"Create in me a clean heart, O God,
And renew a steadfast spirit within me."
(Ps. 51:10)

God requires purity of heart (Ps. 15:1–2), but He also provides for it—through His grace and forgiveness. Through His Word and Spirit. Through prayers of confession and the counsel of other believers. Through Christ Himself.

Is there anything you would like to ask God to scour from your heart?

_____

_____

_____

Do you really believe He has the power and the patience to do it? He does, you know (Phil. 1:6).

_____

_____

_____

Why not tell God specifically what you want Him to do?

_____

_____

_____

Now, what's your part?

_____

_____

_____

What a God we have, who isn't turned off by what He sees in our hearts. Rather, He draws us to Himself and patiently shapes our hearts to match His own. Have you trusted Him yet with your heart?

Digging Deeper

"Oh that someone would give me water to drink from the well of Bethlehem!" David yearned out loud (1 Chron. 11:17). Three of his mighty men heard this, looked at each other, and off they went—breaking through enemy lines to get David his cool drink (v. 18).

That's strong support—the same kind of support God wishes to give those whose hearts are at peace with Him (2 Chron. 16:9).[4]

"Now, wait a minute," you may be thinking. "Are you trying to tell me that God would go so far as to provide *me* a cool drink?"

In a word, yes. Because this idea sounds nice? No. Because God promises it in His Word. Let's take a look.

According to Psalm 23:1–2, where does our Shepherd lead us?

_____

_____

What is His purpose in doing this (v. 3a)?

_____

_____

Does He really care about something so small as a literal drink? Jesus can help you answer that—look at Matthew 10:42 and 25:31–40, especially verse 35. What does He say?

_____

_____

_____

What other thirst does the Lord want to quench for us (see Ps. 42:1–2, 7–8)?

_____

_____

_____

4. The same Hebrew word, *chazaq*, is used of David's mighty men's support (1 Chron. 11:10) and God's support of "those whose hearts are completely His" (2 Chron. 16:9).

And what sort of drink does Jesus want to give us (John 4:13–14)?

_____

_____

_____

It looks as though God *does* care after all, doesn't it? Scripture overflows with His desire to support and refresh His people, slaking our thirsting hearts with His tender kindness and grace. Now the only question is, Will you take the drink He offers?

> Now on the last day, the great day of the feast, Jesus stood and cried out, saying, "If any man is thirsty, let him come to Me and drink. He who believes in Me, as the Scripture said, 'From his innermost being shall flow rivers of living water.'" (John 7:37–38)

Chapter 6

WARNINGS FOR ALL IN LEADERSHIP
2 Chronicles 26

Leading isn't easy, for a variety of reasons. It involves a lot more stress and responsibility. The higher visibility makes you an easy target for those who don't like you or appreciate your style. And the hours aren't always the best.

The most difficult part about leading, though, may be success. Once you're established as a successful leader, a certain amount of recognition, prosperity, and self-confidence comes with the package. Before you know it, you can get impressed with yourself . . . and unimpressed with God. Nineteenth-century preacher Charles H. Spurgeon knew this temptation all too well.

> Success exposes a man to the pressure of people and thus tempts him to hold on to his gains by means of fleshly methods and practices, and to let himself be ruled wholly by the dictatorial demands of incessant expansion. Success can go to my head, and will unless I remember that it is God who accomplishes the work, that He can continue to do so without any help, and that He will be able to make out with other means whenever He cuts me down to size.[1]

If we heed the warnings in this study, maybe we can learn how to handle success in leadership *before* God has to "cut us down to size."

Who's Getting the Glory?

The Creator and Sustainer of the universe says,

> "I am the Lord," that is My name;
> I will not give My glory to another,
> Nor My praise to graven images." (Isa. 42:8)

---

1. Helmut Thielecke, *Encounter with Spurgeon*, (Philadelphia, Pa.: Fortress, 1963), quoted in J. Oswald Sanders, *Spiritual Leadership*, rev. ed. (Chicago, Ill.: Moody Press, 1980), p. 189.

God is protective of His glory, not because He loves the spotlight—like we do—but because He is the only One worthy of it. It is rightfully His (see also Exod. 20:4–5).

How can we tell if we're infringing on God's glory? The first step in answering that question is to get a handle on the meaning of *glory*.

Glory Defined

The most often used Hebrew word for *glory* is *kabod*. Theologian Charles Ryrie describes the thought behind the term and contrasts God's glory with ours:

> The glory of God means the awesomeness, splendor, and importance of God seen in some way. When God is glorified, He is seen or shown in a pure, worthy, and sincere way. With God there can be no showing off with a sense of pride, for His character is perfect, and when He is seen, there is no mixture of wrong motives or sin. When, for example, Isaiah saw the glory of God, it was inseparably linked with the holiness of God: "Holy, holy, holy, is the Lord of hosts, the whole earth is full of His glory" (Isaiah 6:3). With God holiness and glory fit together in total compatibility. With us glory gets tinged with wrong, even sinful, motives.[2]

Glory Stealers

When we fail to acknowledge God's control over our lives, when we try to usurp His authority or take credit for His accomplishments, we steal His glory. Because, like the spectator who tries to get his face on camera, waving his arms behind the athlete being interviewed, we call attention to ourselves instead of God.

Someone has said, "Man is the strangest creature on earth; when you pat him on the back, his head swells." The fleshly urge to puff up with pride accompanies every accomplishment, every accolade, even every unearned benefit. Just consider a few examples from Scripture.

Adam and Eve used their freedom to pursue equality with their Maker (Gen. 3). Saul, Israel's first king, turned his God-given

---

2. Charles C. Ryrie, *Transformed by His Glory* (Wheaton, Ill.: Scripture Press Publications, Victor Books, 1990), p. 18.

position into an avenue for recognition, control, and revenge (1 Sam. 8–26). Solomon, whom God had made wealthy and wise, charted his own course into materialism and self-indulgence (1 Kings 3–11). Nebuchadnezzar, God's tool in disciplining the Israelites, preened himself over *his* Babylon's greatness (Dan. 4). Judas, Jesus' own disciple and close companion, turned Christ's grace into an opportunity to betray Him (Luke 22:47–48). And Satan himself, one of the brightest of God's angels, turned his privilege into a quest for power "like the Most High" (Isa. 14:12–17).

Stealing God's glory isn't always so drastic, though. Sometimes it's simply disregarding God's revealed will and doing things our own way. Like King Uzziah did.

A King Blessed by God

King Uzziah started out as one of those rare kings who "did right in the sight of the Lord" (2 Chron. 26:4), so he received the Lord's special favor.

His Reign

Uzziah's reign was long, prosperous, and characterized by obedience.

> Uzziah was sixteen years old when he became king, and he reigned fifty-two years in Jerusalem; and his mother's name was Jechiliah of Jerusalem. And he did right in the sight of the Lord according to all that his father Amaziah had done. And he continued to seek God in the days of Zechariah, who had understanding through the vision of God; and as long as he sought the Lord, God prospered him. (vv. 3–5)

Would you put a teenager in charge of a kingdom? God did. And Uzziah led Judah until he was sixty-eight. What a career! The only king with a longer reign was Manasseh, who ruled fifty-five years. Let's take a look at Uzziah's accomplishments.

His Accomplishments

Verse 2 tells us Uzziah "built Eloth and restored it to Judah." Also called Ezion-Geber, Eloth was a port city located about 150 miles south of Jerusalem on the northern tip of the present-day Gulf of Aqaba, the eastern finger of the Red Sea. It was not only strategic for trade but also crucial for defending against southern enemies. By reclaiming this ancient city for Judah, Uzziah expanded and strengthened his kingdom.

Also, no one, it seems, could withstand Judah's military might under Uzziah's command.

> Now he went out and warred against the Philistines, and broke down the wall of Gath and the wall of Jabneh and the wall of Ashdod; and he built cities in the area of Ashdod and among the Philistines. And God helped him against the Philistines, and against the Arabians who lived in Gur-baal, and the Meunites. The Ammonites also gave tribute to Uzziah, and his fame extended to the border of Egypt, for he became very strong. (vv. 6–8)

Uzziah was a prolific builder too. He fortified Jerusalem with defense towers (v. 9), took on massive agricultural projects (v. 10), and mustered a well-equipped army with strong weaponry, such as arrow-launchers and catapults (vv. 11–15).

Military success. Agricultural success. Building success. Success domestically and abroad. What a résumé! If Uzziah's press corps had created a slogan for him, it would have read, "Uzziah can't go wrong; His God has made him strong." But he *did* go wrong . . . because he forgot who made him strong.

King Uzziah built many towers and hewed many cisterns (2 Chron. 26:10). This cistern dug by Uzziah is located in Borot Hazaz in the central Negev highlands.

Uzziah loved the soil (2 Chron. 26:10). His many building projects included many vineyards and towers, along with other agricultural works.

A King Bloated with Pride

Uzziah's story takes a self-centered turn in verse 16.

> But when he became strong, his heart was so proud that he acted corruptly, and he was unfaithful to the Lord his God, for he entered the temple of the Lord to burn incense on the altar of incense.

Danger: Power Surge

Somewhere in the course of his reign, Uzziah began to trust his own power instead of the God who empowered him. How very much like us. We reach out for God when we sense our own weakness and inadequacy. Then, after the Lord delivers us, blesses us, and prospers us, we survey all we've gained and sigh a self-satisfying sigh: "I have arrived."

We need to think, believe, and say like the psalmist:

> Not to us, O Lord, not to us,
> But to Thy name give glory
> Because of Thy lovingkindness, because of Thy
>   truth. (Ps. 115:1)

Any strength we have, any greatness we achieve, any righteousness we possess all comes from God's hand of loving-kindness.

Unfortunately, Uzziah was so impressed with himself that he entered the temple to burn incense—a duty reserved solely for priests. This was no small offense. God had specified in His law how He wanted to be approached in worship, and He had more than once punished and even destroyed those who violated His instructions (see Lev. 10:1–3; Num. 16:1–40; 1 Sam. 13:8–14; 15:22–35).

God takes worship seriously, and He shares His glory with no one—not even a successful king like Uzziah.

Consequence: Power Failure

With the censer swinging from his hand, Uzziah soon discovered that even kings can't do everything they want.

> Then Azariah the priest entered after him and with him eighty priests of the Lord, valiant men. And they opposed Uzziah the king and said to him, "It is not for you, Uzziah, to burn incense to the Lord, but for the priests, the sons of Aaron who are consecrated to burn incense. Get out of the sanctuary, for you have been unfaithful, and will have no honor from the Lord God." (2 Chron. 26:17–18)

Illustration of a high priest with a censer. Uzziah engaged in priestly activity and "entered the temple of the Lord to burn incense on the altar of incense" (2 Chron. 26:16). God judged him with leprosy while he still held the censer in his hand, and he remained a leper until he died (v. 21).

Talk about evidence of God's grace! Uzziah had disregarded God's design for worship and defiled the temple. Yet, rather than consuming the king in His wrath, God gave him a chance to heed the priests' rebuke and admit his error. Uzziah's heart, however, had already been hardened by pride, and he responded with rage (v. 19a).

That's an indication, by the way, of how far someone has drifted from the Lord. If an individual heeds godly counsel, you've got something to work with. If, however, a person gets defensive, angry, or tries to rationalize his or her sin, God may have to intervene in a powerful way. Uzziah was a prime candidate for God's discipline.

> And while he was enraged with the priests, the leprosy broke out on his forehead before the priests in the house of the Lord, beside the altar of incense. And Azariah the chief priest and all the priests looked at him, and behold, he was leprous on his forehead; and they hurried him out of there, and he himself also hastened to get out because the Lord had smitten him. (vv. 19b–20)

Now that's how to get someone out of the temple *fast*. Under the Law, lepers were unclean; they weren't allowed near other people, let alone God's holy temple. They had to cry out, "Unclean! Unclean!" to warn others away, and they lived in isolation unless they were healed and purified (see Lev. 13–14, note especially 13:45–46).

What a tragedy! Uzziah lived out the rest of his life in quarantine and died in disgrace (2 Chron. 26:21–23). His leprosy lingered until his burial, a grisly reminder that God shares His glory with no one and that He exalts the humble in *His* time (James 4:6, 10; 1 Pet. 5:6).

Five Warnings for All Leaders

Uzziah's disgrace, though tragic, can be our deliverance, if we'll mark these five warnings that linger from his life.

Beware when the battle within is greater than the battle without. Uzziah might have conquered nations and achieved immeasurable success, but his fiercest battle raged within: He couldn't conquer his pride. Leaders, don't think you have arrived simply because you have amassed wealth, built a successful business or ministry, or collected a gallery of awards. It's the success of the soul that matters most to God. And until that battle's won, the rest doesn't mean much.

Beware when you become more interested in building your own kingdom than God's. When achievement and recognition come, watch out. That's when we're tempted to survey our lofty success and think we're higher than God's law, as Uzziah did. God employs us in the building of *His* kingdom; we don't use God to build ours. If we try the latter, we'd better get ready for a lesson on who's in charge.

Beware when the Lord's help is no longer considered essential. Our conscious dependence on the Lord decreases in direct proportion to the extent that we depend on other things. When we're on top, we tend to forget Him and put our trust in money, buildings, influential people, and slick programs. But His strength and guidance, especially for the leader, are never optional—they're essential.

Beware when reproofs are resisted instead of respected. Proverbs tells us, "He is on the path of life who heeds instruction, But he who forsakes reproof goes astray" (Prov. 10:17). If we think we're above criticism, we'd better check which path we're on, because it's not the path of life. God will get our attention, maybe through some drastic measure, as He did with Uzziah.

Beware when the consequences of sin no longer bring fear. No doubt, Uzziah knew at least some of his nation's history and how God had judged kings and other leaders who had disrespected His holy law. Yet he burned incense in the temple anyway, undeterred by the fear of God's judgment. Like drunk drivers who never think they'll lose control of their cars, leaders who ignore consequences are capable of doing great damage to themselves and others.

So lead on. But lead with humility. And let God take care of the glory. He's the only One who deserves it . . . and the only One who can handle it.

Living Insights

The best way to keep from stealing God's glory is to remain thankful for all He provides. By reminding ourselves that everything, even success, comes from Him, we sidestep the snare of pride.

Take some time to make a list of God's faithful blessings in your life. Start by reflecting on the grace and mercy He has given you through the death and resurrection of His dear Son. What hope of

50

"soul success" would we have, had Christ not taken our sin on Himself, died in our place, and given us His perfect righteousness?

_____

_____

_____

Now move on to the relationships that enrich your life. How have these people extended God's warm embrace and encouraging words to you? What lessons about living have you learned from them? How would your life be different if they weren't here?

_____

_____

_____

How about your health, abilities, interests, and special talents?

_____

_____

_____

Next, think about your material possessions. What things has God entrusted to your care so that you can more fully enjoy life?

_____

_____

_____

Whenever you're tempted to take credit for any of these blessings, come back to this page and remember this:

> Every good thing bestowed and every perfect gift is
> from above, coming down from the Father of lights,
> with whom there is no variation, or shifting shadow.
> (James 1:17)

God may not share His glory, but He's mighty generous with everything else.

Chapter 7

THE EXIT OF A NATION
2 Kings 17

How far does your patience extend? Before answering, consider
these questions:

- How many times do you let someone get away with the same
  offense?

- How often do you allow your child to disobey your instructions
  before you spank or take away privileges?

- At what point is chronic tardiness grounds for dismissing one
  of your employees?

- And how many times can a person lie to you before losing your
  trust?

Perhaps you're not as patient as you thought you were—which
may not be all bad. Certainly, patience is a godly trait, one of the
fruits of the Spirit (see Gal. 5:22). But patience becomes
permissiveness—even irresponsibility—when we allow someone to
sin continually, put themselves in harm's way, or take advantage of
us. Why? Because God has instilled in us a sense of what is right
and wrong, proper and improper. Sooner or later, we all reach a
point where we say, "Enough is enough."

If we who are tainted with sin get upset when our instructions
are ignored; imagine how God, who is perfect, holy, and pure, feels
when we disobey Him. He has every right to require us to live in
a way that reflects His truth and His character; so He demands our
obedience. Yes, God is brimming with love, grace, forgiveness, and
mercy. But He will not sit idly by, whistling away the hours while
His people thumb their noses at Him. At some point, even God
says, "Enough is enough."

When God's patience ran out with Israel, He sent the Assyrians
to sack the capital city and enslave the Israelites. As we study the
northern kingdom's last days as a nation, recorded in 2 Kings 17,
we'll discover that God, though long-suffering, takes obedience
seriously. And so should we.

Warnings from the Prophets

"How could God send a godless nation to plunder His own people?" some might ask. "Isn't that a little extreme?" On the contrary. What's amazing is that God put off the Assyrian invasion as long as He did. Time and time again, He had sent His spokesmen, the prophets, to call the people to repentance and to return to Him. Time and time again, the people refused to listen.

Elijah

You would think Israel would have grasped God's message during Elijah's ministry. It was Elijah who confronted King Ahab face-to-face about his abandoning God's laws and worshiping Baal (1 Kings 18:17–18); then he called on God to display His consuming power on Mount Carmel (vv. 30–39). Yet, even after God's fire fell from heaven, and even after the deaths of 450 prophets of Baal (v. 40), the nation continued on its path of wickedness.

Elisha

Then came Elisha, Elijah's protégé (2 Kings 2–9, 13). Elisha's ministry, as Merrill F. Unger points out, differed in temperament from that of his mentor.

> Elijah was a man whose mission was to accuse of sin or bring judgment upon men because of it. Elisha, while defending the ancient religion, comes as the healer, and so his miracles were those of restoring to life, increasing the widow's oil, making pure the bitter waters. There is tender sympathy for friends, tears for his country's prospective woes. And yet there is firmness in maintaining the right, sternness of judgment, and seeming forgetfulness of self.[1]

Though some might consider Elisha's ministry less dramatic or confrontational than Elijah's, he was nonetheless a constant presence of God's holiness, compassion, and righteousness in a nation that continued to sin against the Lord.

Jonah

And who could forget Jonah, that reluctant prophet who ran

---

1. Merrill F. Unger, *Unger's Bible Dictionary,* 3d ed. (Chicago, Ill.: Moody Press, 1966), p. 309.

from God and found himself in the belly of a fish? God used him to turn the hearts of the pagan Ninevites to Himself. Though Nineveh repented, Israel did not. They persisted in rebellion even during Jonah's ministry.

Amos

Amos, the simple shepherd from Tekoah, was called by God to bring Israel's sins to light during Jeroboam's reign.

> Thus says the Lord,
> "For three transgressions of Israel and for four
> I will not revoke its punishment,
> Because they sell the righteous for money
> And the needy for a pair of sandals.
> These who pant after the very dust of the earth on
> the head of the helpless
> Also turn aside the way of the humble;
> And a man and his father resort to the same girl
> In order to profane My holy name.
> And on garments taken as pledges they stretch out
> beside every altar,
> And in the house of their God they drink the wine
> of those who have been fined." (Amos 2:6–8)

Amos predicted the king's death and Israel's captivity (7:11). Rather than heeding his message and turning to God, though, the religious leaders tried to get rid of Amos (vv. 12–13).

Hosea

God commanded Hosea to marry a prostitute to picture how Israel had forsaken the Lord and committed adultery with the gods of other nations (Hos. 1:2). From violence to idolatry, the people's sins multiplied, intensifying their stubborn refusal to repent (see chap. 4). So Hosea, too, predicted the Assyrian invasion.

> They will not return to the land of Egypt;
> But Assyria—he will be their king,
> Because they refused to return to Me.
> And the sword will whirl against their cities,
> And will demolish their gate bars
> And consume them because of their counsels.
> So My people are bent on turning from Me.

Though they call them to the One on high,
None at all exalts Him.
(Hos. 11:5–7; see also 8:1–9)

Prophet after prophet, all with different personalities and back-grounds, yet all with the same message for Israel: "Repent, and God will forgive. Continue in sin, and God will judge." The prophets' words, though offering God's freedom and grace, annoyed Israel's kings and priests like a fly at a banquet.

Would you allow someone to ignore your instructions that long—209 years—without taking action?

Signs of the Times

Not only did the people of Israel disregard the words of the prophets, they ignored repeated signs that their relationship with God was hanging on a thin and fraying thread.

Wicked Leaders

In little more than two centuries, nineteen kings had sat on Israel's throne. All of them were bad. Yet the people followed them; the priests served them. Few were the voices that condemned sin, championed righteousness, and called the nation back to the Lord. Israel had drifted so far from the glow of God's holiness that the tarnished crowns of her kings became her guiding light.

Wicked leadership doesn't make for a spiritually healthy nation, as Proverbs says:

When the righteous increase, the people rejoice,
But when a wicked man rules, people groan.
(Prov. 29:2; see also vv. 4, 12)

When our leaders show signs of drifting from God, we should make them aware of it and seek the Lord more diligently than ever. If we don't, we run the risk of patterning our lives after the world and incurring God's discipline.

Indifference to God's Commands

Had the people of Israel learned from history—from the time of the judges, from Saul, from Solomon, from Ahab and Jezebel, from each wicked king onward—they would have known that God doesn't tolerate disobedience indefinitely. They would have known that their continued resistance to His clear commands would bring destruction.

Yet the Lord warned Israel and Judah, through all His prophets and every seer, saying, "Turn from your evil ways and keep My commandments, My statutes according to all the law which I commanded your fathers, and which I sent to you through My servants the prophets." However, they did not listen, but stiffened their neck like their fathers, who did not believe in the Lord their God. And they rejected His statutes and His covenant which He made with their fathers, and His warnings with which He warned them. And they followed vanity and became vain, and went after the nations which surrounded them, concerning which the Lord had commanded them not to do like them. And they forsook all the commandments of the Lord their God and made for themselves molten images, even two calves, and made an Asherah and worshiped all the host of heaven and served Baal. Then they made their sons and their daughters pass through the fire, and prac- ticed divination and enchantments, and sold them- selves to do evil in the sight of the Lord, provoking Him. So the Lord was very angry with Israel, and removed them from His sight; none was left except the tribe of Judah. (2 Kings 17:13–18)

God gave us His Word to follow, not because He delights in mechanical servitude, but because He knows what's best for us. And His Word will never steer us wrong. If we consistently ignore His commands, though, we only make life harder for ourselves.

Adopting the Practices of Other Nations

Israel's abandonment of God's Word led them to embrace the values of neighboring pagan countries. They

> walked in the customs of the nations whom the Lord had driven out before the sons of Israel, and in the customs of the kings of Israel which they had intro- duced. (v. 8)

Following God is a lifestyle, not just a casual notion (see Deut. 6:4–9). But when we are no longer focusing on Him, our attention latches on to something else. And that something else defines and directs our life, leading us in inferior and destructive ways.

Rarely, though, do we abandon God overnight, on a whim. We begin slowly, telling ourselves that this little sin will do no harm. Then we become comfortable with it. And when we discover that our loving God doesn't zap us every time we disobey Him, we stop fearing His judgment; we stop caring about what He thinks. Solomon knew all too well our tendency to embrace evil when God gives us room.

> Because the sentence against an evil deed is not executed quickly, therefore the hearts of the sons of men among them are given fully to do evil.
> (Eccles. 8:11)

Over time, Israel drifted further and further away from God. Then they presumed upon His patience and conformed to the image of the surrounding nations.

Sleeping with the Enemy

Though God planted Israel in the midst of unbelieving Gentile lands, He never wanted them to lose their distinctiveness as a holy people. They were supposed to be different from those nations, a people who trusted their Deliverer and Provider in every situation—spiritual, physical, political, or military. But Israel's leaders repeatedly turned away from God to seek strength in human relationships, including alliances with their enemies. How ironic, then, that God chose a pagan nation to exact His judgment.

> In the twelfth year of Ahaz king of Judah, Hoshea the son of Elah became king over Israel in Samaria, and reigned nine years. And he did evil in the sight of the Lord, only not as the kings of Israel who were before him. Shalmaneser king of Assyria came up against him, and Hoshea became his servant and paid him tribute. But the king of Assyria found conspiracy in Hoshea, who had sent messengers to So king of Egypt and had offered no tribute to the king of Assyria, as he had done year by year; so the king of Assyria shut him up and bound him in prison. Then the king of Assyria invaded the whole land and went up to Samaria and besieged it three years. In the ninth year of Hoshea, the king

of Assyria captured Samaria and carried Israel away into exile to Assyria, and settled them in Halah and Habor, on the river of Gozan, and in the cities of the Medes. (2 Kings 17:1–6)

Samaria, the capital of the northern kingdom. "And the sons of Israel walked in all the sins of Jeroboam . . . until the Lord removed Israel from His sight, as He spoke through all His servants the prophets. So Israel was carried away into exile from their own land to Assyria" (2 Kings 17:22–23).

Hoshea could have called on God to defeat the Assyrians. Instead, he sought help from Egypt—evidence of how far Israel had drifted. King Hoshea hadn't yet learned that the only secure alliance is with the Lord God Almighty. Not learning that lesson cost him his throne . . . and the freedom of his nation. G. Frederick Owen describes the last days of Israel.

> Hoshea prepared for a long siege with the hope of receiving help from Egypt, but for this he looked in vain. The siege of Samaria continued for two years—724 to 722 B.C.—under Shalmaneser V; then Sargon II, his successor, continued it for another year. At last Samaria's heights were stormed, King Hoshea was led away to spend the rest of his life in an Assyrian prison, and the people were deported to Assyria where they were sent to various sections of the country to be absorbed by the people

among whom they dwelt, or finally to journey to other lands.[2]

What a tragedy! The descendants of Abraham, chosen by God to be His own possession and to inhabit the Promised Land . . . now snatched from their homes and enslaved by a godless people. So the northern kingdom of Israel fell, absorbed into the expanding kingdom of Assyria.

Four Enduring Lessons

What can we learn from Israel's tragedy? First, *we must open our ears* to God's warnings and not take them lightly. He means what He says. Second, *we must open our eyes* to what's happening around us and be on the lookout for spiritual deterioration in our lives. Third, *we must open our mouths* to contend for the truth and communicate it clearly so this generation and the next will take God seriously. Fourth and finally, *we must open our hearts*. We must give God reign in everything we think and do so He can shape us into His image. Only when we allow our hearts to be taken captive by the Lord are we truly free.

Living Insights

We will never be enslaved by the Assyrians, but that doesn't mean we can't go into exile. Spiritual exile, that is. Just as disobedience brought physical captivity and geographical separation from God's blessings for the Israelites, it brings spiritual enslavement and separation for us today. Sin hinders our fellowship with God and keeps us from enjoying all He has given us in Christ.

If we ignore God's Word, neglect our areas of vulnerability, and adopt the world's way of thinking and living, it won't be long before the Enemy is scaling the walls of our hearts.

What kind of shape is your spiritual fortress in today? Could it withstand an attack from Satan?

_____

_____

2. G. Frederick Owen, *Abraham to the Middle-East Crisis*, 4th ed., rev. (Grand Rapids, Mich.: William B. Eerdmans Publishing Co., 1957), p. 70.

What cracks in the walls do you see? What weaknesses need to be reinforced?

_____

_____

If the Enemy were to attack you right now, where do you think he would strike?

_____

_____

In whom (or what) are you trusting for your protection? Do you know the Savior well enough to have complete confidence in His strength? Are you obeying your Commander?

_____

_____

In what way is the Word of God standing guard over your heart?

_____

_____

What steps can you take to make your heart more resistant to attack?

_____

_____

Remember, changes can take time. So be patient with yourself. Satan can invade a fortress through the window of unrealistic expectations too.

Chapter 8

JUST A CHUNK
OF BRONZE
2 Kings 18:1–4; Numbers 21:4–9

Hitler wanted it. And he would spare no expense to find it.

The Führer had soldiers, spies, and archaeologists crawling like ants all over Cairo, digging up the desert looking for it. It was there somewhere; he knew it. When they found it, the war would be as good as over. For against this weapon there was no defense. It was supernatural, otherworldly. And with its power in his hands, Hitler's Third Reich would rule the world.

Unfortunately for Hitler, he neglected one essential fact: The ark of the covenant was no weapon, no paranormal bazooka to be wielded by the first tyrant to unearth it. True, the ark had displayed great power among the Israelites. But the power resided in God, not the ark itself, as the Nazis in *Raiders of the Lost Ark* discovered in that film's final climactic scene. In one terrifying moment, God flashed his omnipotence like a sword in battle and consumed Hitler's henchmen in a firestorm of judgment.

Those who seek power, comfort, protection, or salvation in religious relics—even the ones used by God—be warned. God allows no substitutes. Although certain symbols *represent* Him, they cannot *replace* Him. God alone must be the focus of our worship. If He's not, whatever takes His place becomes an idol.

King Hezekiah of Judah knew this all too well. During his reign, he destroyed the images of pagan gods and goddesses along with the bronze serpent God had used to deliver the Israelites from death during Moses' day. So intent were the people of Judah on worshiping in their own way that they had taken the metal snake—once an instrument of God's salvation—and made it a god itself.

What happened? How did God's people twist what He had used for good into an object of idolatry? Let's go back before Hezekiah's reign—seven hundred years before—to the days of Moses. We'll examine the origin of the bronze serpent and discover how the people got so far off track. Then maybe we can keep the same thing from happening in our own lives.

61

The Beginning of the Story

What more could the children of Israel ask for? God had freed them from Pharaoh's cruel bondage and miraculously delivered them through the Red Sea. He led them with a cloud by day and a pillar of fire by night. He covered the wilderness with a crust of fresh manna every morning and caused water to flow from rocks. He organized them into a nation and gave them His laws.

So how did they respond to God's faithful protection and provision? With thanksgiving, worship, and obedience? Hardly. You might say the Israelites had the gift of complaining. And they used it frequently.

A Bunch of Complainers

Then they set out from Mount Hor by the way of the Red Sea, to go around the land of Edom; and the people became impatient because of the journey. And the people spoke against God and Moses, "Why have you brought us up out of Egypt to die in the wilderness? For there is no food and no water, and we loathe this miserable food." (Num. 21:4–5)

An amazing complaint, considering that God had just provided water for them from a rock at Meribah (20:11). And "this miserable food"? That was the manna, which the psalmist recognized as "food from heaven," "the bread of angels" (Ps. 78:24–25). Their gripes weren't reasonable. The Israelites were simply tired of wandering in the wilderness and having to trust God for everything. They craved the comfort and predictability of slavery in Egypt and detested the hard way of holiness. Just as we do sometimes.

Well, God had heard enough. It was time to let the Israelites feel the stinging results of their own sinfulness.

A Pack of Snakes

And the Lord sent fiery serpents among the people and they bit the people, so that many people of Israel died. (Num. 21:6)

Nothing like a camp full of slithering adders to get your attention! *Fiery* may refer to the painful bite the snakes inflicted, or it could also describe their color, which might have been red, yellow, or orange.

Lest you think this judgment too severe for mere whining, consider the seriousness of Israel's grumbling. They weren't just bewailing their conditions; they were rejecting God's care and provision. Their faith should have been inexhaustible by this point—how many times had they seen God work? Yet so faithless were the Israelites that they would have swapped the Promised Land for a slave's supper. In essence, God's kindness wasn't good enough for them, so He let them feel His wrath.

Knowing that Moses had God's ear, the Israelites begged their leader to intercede.

> So the people came to Moses and said, "We have sinned, because we have spoken against the Lord and you; intercede with the Lord, that He may remove the serpents from us." And Moses interceded for the people. (v. 7)

If we were in God's place, we might not care what happened to such ungrateful people. Fortunately for the Israelites, though, God's ways are higher and more merciful than ours (Isa. 55:6–9).

A Hope of Recovery

> Then the Lord said to Moses, "Make a fiery serpent, and set it on a standard; and it shall come about, that everyone who is bitten, when he looks at it, he shall live." (Num. 21:8)

God responded with grace and provided the antitoxin for the venom coursing through the Hebrews' veins. But wasn't it a strange remedy? Nevertheless, it was the only plan God provided. So Moses obeyed. He crafted a serpent—no doubt with the help of some of the artisans who had constructed the tent of meeting—attached it to a pole, and raised it high above the heads of the people.

> And Moses made a bronze serpent and set it on the standard; and it came about, that if a serpent bit any man, when he looked to the bronze serpent, he lived. (v. 9)

Just imagine yourself as a dying Israelite that day. Your head is spinning. Your vision is blurring. The fang wounds on your legs and arms burn like fire. And your strength drains as your heart pumps the poison throughout your circulatory system. You're about to lie facedown in the dirt and wait for death, when you hear someone shout, "Look! Look up at the serpent and live!" With one last desperate motion, you hold up your head and see something hoisted high in the air, glinting in the sun—a sculpted snake. Your strength returns and the pain disappears. God has given you a second chance at life.

Sounds a lot like salvation, doesn't it? It's meant to. The incident of the fiery serpents, like many events in the Old Testament, foreshadowed the substitutionary death of Christ. All of us are born with sin's deadly poison coursing through our spiritual veins; we're destined for eternal death. Our only hope for salvation is to look up to the One who hung on the cross. He has taken our sin on Himself and given us His righteousness so that we might be delivered from eternal death and live a new life pleasing to God.

Do you remember what Jesus told Nicodemus?

> "And as Moses lifted up the serpent in the wilderness, even so must the Son of Man be lifted up; that whoever believes may in Him have eternal life." (John 3:14–15)

Back in the wilderness, you would think that, after witnessing such a dramatic deliverance, the children of Israel would never again forget their God. But they did. Over time the bronze serpent, the very symbol of their salvation, coiled around their hearts and became an object of worship.

The Rest of the Story

Now let's jump ahead seven hundred years. King Hezekiah, not Moses, is the leader. The southern kingdom of Judah, not the wilderness, is the setting. There are no real snakes. But the land is staggering from the poison of idolatry.

A King Who Did Right

When Hezekiah came to the throne, he wasted no time instituting reform in Judah.

> Now it came about in the third year of Hoshea, the son of Elah king of Israel, that Hezekiah the son of Ahaz king of Judah became king. He was twenty-five years old when he became king, and he reigned twenty-nine years in Jerusalem; and his mother's

name was Abi the daughter of Zechariah. And he did right in the sight of the Lord, according to all that his father David had done. He removed the high places and broke down the sacred pillars and cut down the Asherah. (2 Kings 18:1–4a)

The "high places" were sites on mountains chosen for offering sacrifice and incense to pagan gods. Asherah were wooden symbols of female deity. Hezekiah went after them all. And he didn't stop there.

An Idol That Needed to Be Destroyed

He also broke in pieces the bronze serpent that Moses had made, for until those days the sons of Israel burned incense to it; and it was called Nehu-shtan. (v. 4b)

Some leaders might have been satisfied with destroying the overtly pagan idols. But the serpent? "Well, that's part of our spiritual heritage. That has connection to Jehovah," some might have protested. "Surely there's no harm in letting that cult thrive." Hezekiah, however, saw the harm clearly. He understood that the worship of the serpent was an affront to God; it clearly violated His law (Exod. 20:3–4). The people had even given the serpent a name, Nehushtan.[1]

Some superstitious Israelite had apparently hung onto that snake in the wilderness. As it, along with stories of the fiery serpent, crept its way down through the generations, a cult developed around the reptile and its legendary power. And the fame of a snake supplanted faith in God.

Thank God for a man like Hezekiah, who was willing to destroy the idol and upset the status quo in order to honor his Lord. No wonder "the Lord was with him; wherever he went he prospered" (2 Kings 18:7).

---

1. "Nehushtan was . . . a word that sounded like the Hebrew for 'bronze,' 'snake,' and 'unclean thing.'" Thomas L. Constable, "2 Kings," in *The Bible Knowledge Commentary*, Old Testament edition, ed. John F. Walvoord and Roy B. Zuck (Wheaton, Ill.: Scripture Press Publications, Victor Books, 1985), p. 573.

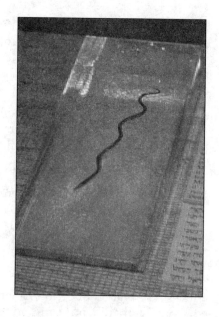

This copper serpent dating from the twelfth century B.C. was discovered in an Egyptian temple at the Timnah copper mines in southern Israel.

And What about Us?

If you don't worship a snake on a stick—or burn incense to Buddha, pray to statues, or discover silhouettes of Jesus in your pancakes—you may think you're free from the temptation of relic-worship. But no one is. We all have to watch what we allow to capture our thoughts, our time, and our trust.

Your "chunk of bronze" may be a graveside. Maybe you keep visiting that memorial to do more than grieve or reflect on your life with your loved one. Perhaps you're somehow seeking that person's help or hoping they'll put in a good word for you with God. If so, you've made the burial site a kind of idol to which you return with ritualistic regularity. You've substituted your loved one for Christ, your true Intercessor.

Your Nehushtan might even be a crucifix. Do you feel that wearing a cross around your neck or carrying one in your pocket will deflect evil? There's nothing wrong with crosses; the Cross of Christ, after all, is the axis on which our theology turns. We display crosses in our churches and homes to remind us of the Lord Jesus Christ, the price He paid for our sins, and His abounding love for us. But it's the Savior, not the symbol, who protects us and keeps us from sin.

Ironically, even the Bible can distract us from God if used superstitiously. A home isn't protected from catastrophe simply because a dusty Bible sits on a corner table. And religious trinkets hanging from our rear-view mirror don't insulate us from accidents. God gave us His Word so we could study it and know *Him*. He gave us symbols to remind us of *Him*.

Satan is so crafty, he'll even try to convince us to turn our churches into idols. Too often, we make buildings the priority, programs the measure of success. We take our most charismatic and popular leaders and lift them high above the people in order to attract numbers.

There's only one way to keep the Nehushtans of the world from slithering up the priority pole and taking the place of God. And that's to keep "fixing our eyes on Jesus, the author and perfecter of faith, who for the joy set before Him endured the cross, despising the shame, and has sat down at the right hand of the throne of God" (Heb. 12:2).

No chunk of bronze ever did that.

Living Insights

It's not always the obvious evil that distracts us from God. Sometimes it's the stuff that looks spiritual. Satan knows that if he wants to dupe Christians, he has to make us think we're doing something good. That's why he "disguises himself as an angel of light" (2 Cor. 11:14). You might even say he sparkles like a bronze serpent.

Is there anything in your life that's drawing your attention away from the Savior? Take some time before the Lord to examine your life—review your schedule, inspect your relationships, consider your goals.

Do you see any warning signs? Any relationships that are taking a priority over your walk with God? Maybe you've unwittingly allowed a pastor, discipler, counselor, even your spouse to become more important to you than Christ Himself. Are you logging more hours watching Christian television or listening to Christian radio programs than you are in the Word? Have you bought the delusion that church busyness automatically equals spiritual growth? Maybe you need to drop out of one of your church committees and spend some time writing in a prayer journal. What do you see in your life?

_____

_____

_____

Did you find any bronze serpents that need to be smashed? If so, how will you do it?

_____

_____

_____

_____

Some idols break easier than others, so don't get discouraged if it takes some consistent hammering. You'll get there, because you have God on your side. And no idol, as Jeremiah told us, is a match for the God of the universe.

> "The customs of the peoples are delusion;
> Because it is wood cut from the forest,
> The work of the hands of a craftsman with a
>   cutting tool.
> They decorate it with silver and with gold;
> They fasten it with nails and with hammers
> So that it will not totter.
> Like a scarecrow in a cucumber field are they,
> And they cannot speak;
> They must be carried,
> Because they cannot walk!
> Do not fear them,
> For they can do no harm,
> Nor can they do any good." . . .
> But the Lord is the true God;
> He is the living God and the everlasting King.
> At His wrath the earth quakes,
> And the nations cannot endure His
>   indignation.

Thus you shall say to them, "The gods that did not make the heavens and the earth shall perish from the earth and from under the heavens."
It is He who made the earth by His power,
Who established the world by His wisdom;
And by His understanding He has stretched out the heavens.
When He utters His voice, there is a tumult of waters in the heavens,
And He causes the clouds to ascend from the end of the earth;
He makes lightning for the rain,
And brings out the wind from His storehouses.
(Jer. 10:3–5, 10–13)

Chapter 9

LIKE FATHER, LIKE SON?
2 Kings 21; 2 Chronicles 33

God has no grandchildren.

That means our children, regardless of how much godly influence we provide for them, must decide for themselves whether they will follow God. There is no such thing as salvation by proxy. Parents can cultivate their children's spiritual sensitivity, but one generation cannot secure regeneration for another.

Case in point: Hezekiah and Manasseh. Godly King Hezekiah had a terribly ungodly son in Manasseh. They were as different as diamonds and dirt. What happened? Let's turn up the soil of Scripture to find out.

A Father-Son Study

If we dig a little deeper into the lives of Hezekiah and Manasseh, we'll unearth some insights we can use to encourage spiritual growth in our families.

A Quick Glance at the Dad

You may remember from our last study that King Hezekiah valiantly purged Judah of idols (2 Kings 18:4). He "did right in the sight of the Lord, according to all that his father David had done" (v. 3). And he earned the reputation as one who

> trusted in the Lord, the God of Israel; so that after him there was none like him among all the kings of Judah, nor among those who were before him. For he clung to the Lord; he did not depart from following Him, but kept His commandments, which the Lord had commanded Moses. And the Lord was with him; wherever he went he prospered. (vv. 5–7a)

Not that Hezekiah was perfect; he wasn't. But his life was characterized by a trust in God and a desire to please Him. In fact, his good character provided a basis for him to approach God and ask Him to heal him of a terminal illness.

> In those days Hezekiah became mortally ill. And
> Isaiah the prophet the son of Amoz came to him
> and said to him, "Thus says the Lord, 'Set your house
> in order, for you shall die and not live.'" (20:1)

How's that for getting straight to the point? "Hope your will is
made out, pal; you're practically history." In response, Hezekiah went
to the same place we all go when we receive such news—to the Lord.

> Then he turned his face to the wall, and prayed to
> the Lord, saying, "Remember now, O Lord, I beseech
> Thee, how I have walked before Thee in truth and
> with a whole heart, and have done what is good in
> Thy sight." And Hezekiah wept bitterly. (vv. 2–3)

In His compassion, God heard Hezekiah's prayer, cured his dis-
ease, and did for him something He hadn't done for anyone else in
Scripture:

> """And I will add fifteen years to your life, and I
> will deliver you and this city from the hand of the
> king of Assyria; and I will defend this city for My
> own sake and for My servant David's sake.""" Then
> Isaiah said, "Take a cake of figs." And they took and
> laid it on the boil, and he recovered. (vv. 6–7)

What would you do if you knew you had exactly fifteen more
years to live? Take a cruise? Dispense with that frustrating diet once
and for all? Share the gospel more often? J. Sidlow Baxter believes
that Hezekiah turned his attention to the arrangement and trans-
mission of the Old Testament Scriptures. He concludes that

> Hezekiah formed a *guild* of men specially set apart
> for such devout literary work. They are called "the
> men of Hezekiah." It is quite clear, for instance, that
> these "men of Hezekiah" had a good hand in the
> shaping of the Book of Proverbs into its present
> form. Turn to Proverbs [25:1], which marks the third
> of the three main divisions of that book. It says
> "These also are proverbs of Solomon, which the men
> of Hezekiah, king of Judah, copied out."[1]

---

1. J. Sidlow Baxter, *Mark These Men* (Grand Rapids, Mich.: Zondervan Publishing House,
1960), p. 126.

Baxter points out another, more cryptic, clue of Hezekiah's involvement in the preservation of the sacred text. He writes,

> At the end of many of the books of the Old Testament, in the Hebrew originals, three capital letters are found. . . . No Hebrew transcriber and no compositor has dared to omit these three capital letters, even though not knowing their meaning. And so, although no one can tell us how they came to be there, or what they mean for certain, they still stand there, even to this day, transcribed and transmitted both in the manuscripts and even in the printed editions of the Hebrew Scriptures. . . . They are the three Hebrew letters, Heth, Zayin, Qoph—in English, H, Z, K. These three letters are the first three in the Hebrew name of Hezekiah, and would well stand for an abbreviation of his name, in the same way that men put their *initials* on documents today. The late Dr. James W. Thirtle weightily suggested that nothing is more reasonable than to believe that when "the men of Hezekiah" completed their work of transcribing the different books, Hezekiah himself should have affixed his own sign-manual at the end, thus confirming their work by royal guarantee.[2]

If this is true, and if during his final fifteen years Hezekiah continued the ambitious building programs, the accumulation of wealth, and the international diplomacy that characterized his earlier life (see 2 Chron. 32:27–30), he may have had little time to oversee the spiritual development of his family. And it was during these final fifteen years that Manasseh was born.[3]

---

2. Baxter, Mark These Men, p. 127.

3. Hezekiah was twenty-five when he assumed the throne of Judah, and he reigned for twenty-nine years (2 Kings 18:2; 2 Chron. 29:1). This means he died at the age of fifty-four. Manasseh began his reign when he was twelve (2 Kings 21:1; 2 Chron. 33:1). So if we subtract twelve from fifty-four—Hezekiah's age at his death—we get forty-two. That's how old Hezekiah was when Manasseh was born. Hezekiah was thirty-nine when he heard he had fifteen years to live. So Manasseh was born three years after this announcement, probably during the height of Hezekiah's productivity.

A Sad Analysis of the Son

Let's be careful not to heap all the blame on Hezekiah for how Manasseh turned out. We're all responsible for our own choices. But if Hezekiah was not around to curb his son's bent toward wickedness, you can see how a twelve-year-old king with no spiritual discipline could lead a nation astray. And that's just what Manasseh did.

> Manasseh was twelve years old when he became king, and he reigned fifty-five years in Jerusalem; and his mother's name was Hephzibah. And he did evil in the sight of the Lord, according to the abominations of the nations whom the Lord dispossessed before the sons of Israel. (2 Kings 21:1–2; see also 2 Chron. 33:1–2)

It seems that Manasseh's mission in life was to undo all the good his father had done. With his appetite for evil unsatisfied by man-made images, Manasseh also worshiped the sun, moon, stars, and planets. He made gods out of creation and ignored the Creator. That would have been enough. But Manasseh's black cloud of wickedness darkened even the holiest of places—the Lord's temple.

> And he built altars in the house of the Lord, of which the Lord had said, "In Jerusalem I will put My name." For he built altars for all the host of heaven in the two courts of the house of the Lord. (vv. 4–5; see also 2 Chron. 33:4–5)

As inanimate objects took on life for Manasseh, the importance of real life diminished. He even valued his gods above the lives of his own sons, whom he offered in sacrifice.

> And he made his sons pass through the fire in the valley of Ben-hinnom; and he practiced witchcraft, used divination, practiced sorcery, and dealt with mediums and spiritists. He did much evil in the sight of the Lord, provoking Him to anger. (2 Chron. 33:6; see also 2 Kings 21:6)

And the living God, who had established a covenant of love with His people, became little more than a religious trinket on a shelf full of carved idols.

73

It seemed that Manasseh set out to undo all the good his father, Hezekiah, had done. This fertility goddess is indicative of the idolatry prevalent during Manasseh's reign.

Then he set the carved image of Asherah that he had made, in the house of which the Lord said to David and to his son Solomon, "In this house and in Jerusalem, which I have chosen from all the tribes of Israel, I will put My name forever. And I will not make the feet of Israel wander anymore from the land which I gave their fathers, if only they will observe to do according to all that I have commanded them, and according to all the law that My servant Moses commanded them." But they did not listen, and Manasseh seduced them to do evil more than the nations whom the Lord destroyed before the sons of Israel. . . .

Moreover, Manasseh shed very much innocent blood until he had filled Jerusalem from one end to another; besides his sin with which he made Judah sin, in doing evil in the sight of the Lord.[4] (2 Kings 21:7–9, 16; see also 2 Chron. 33:7–9)

---

4. According to Herbert Lockyer, "Legend has it that [the prophet Isaiah] was placed inside a hollow tree and sawn asunder at the command of Manasseh (Heb. 11:37)." *All the Men of the Bible* (Grand Rapids, Mich.: Zondervan Publishing House, 1958), p. 158.

The solitary bright spot in Manasseh's life came when he humbled himself before God after being judged by Him (2 Chron. 33:10–13). He instigated a brief period of reform (vv. 14–16), but even the renewed worship of God was tainted by pagan practices (v. 17).

Manasseh's lifetime of disobedience eventually brought the destruction of Jerusalem and enslavement by the Babylonians, just as God had predicted (2 Kings 21:10–15).

Why the Difference?

What a tragedy. Manasseh will be remembered primarily for unraveling the tapestry of godliness his father had woven and tying the nation of Judah into a tangled web of wickedness. Later in 2 Kings we see the ultimate results of his reign.

> In [Jehoiakim's] days Nebuchadnezzar king of Babylon came up, and Jehoiakim became his servant for three years; then he turned and rebelled against him. And the Lord sent against him bands of Chaldeans, bands of Arameans, bands of Moabites, and bands of Ammonites. So He sent them against Judah to destroy it, according to the word of the Lord, which He had spoken through His servants the prophets. Surely at the command of the Lord it came upon Judah to remove them from His sight because of the sins of Manasseh, according to all that he had done, and also for the innocent blood which he shed, for he filled Jerusalem with innocent blood; and the Lord would not forgive. (24:1–4)

Quite a different epitaph from that of his father Hezekiah. Why? What could have made this father and son such radical opposites? Here are three suggestions.

Personally, Manasseh refused to listen and respond to the Lord (2 Chron. 33:10). Each person is held accountable for his own choices. A father cannot obey the Lord for his son. If we refuse to follow the Lord's will, we will face the consequences, regardless of how we were raised.

Relationally, Manasseh was influenced by ungodly associations. His wicked acts were copied from the "abominations of the nations whom the Lord dispossessed before the sons of Israel" (2 Kings 21:2). Manasseh took his cues from the pagan nations that occupied the land before the Hebrews. Today, too, God's people are surrounded by a variety of philosophies that claim to have "the answer." Many of them look good; they provide immediate gratification and earthly comfort. But none of them can take the place of the real spiritual life found in union with God's Son.

Parentally, it's possible that Manasseh was neglected by his father, Hezekiah. Scripture doesn't detail Hezekiah's relationship with Manasseh. But if Hezekiah neglected his son in order to manage his kingdom, accomplish his many building projects, accumulate wealth, and even organize the Scriptures, it's easy to see how Manasseh could grow up a rebel.

A Few Lessons for Parents Today

You may not be worried about passing down a kingdom to your children. But you probably want to influence your family and leave behind a model of godliness for your children to follow if they choose to do so. Let's wrap up with a few lessons on how to work toward leaving such a legacy.

Teach Personal Responsibility

Manasseh had no excuse for his actions other than his own willful disobedience. Ever since Adam said to God, "It was the woman," we've been trying to blame others for our sins. We may not be able to choose how others treat us, but we can choose to respond in responsible ways. We need to teach our children to be proactive and take responsibility for their own actions.

Emphasize the Erosion Principle

Character and integrity erode over time, not in an instant. The kings of Israel and Judah didn't just wake up one day and decide to rebel against God. There had been a history of disregarding God's law, assimilating the idolatry of neighboring nations, and trusting the strength of men instead of the sovereignty of God.

The only thing we need do to insure the erosion of righteousness is . . . nothing. That's right. Just let things go on as usual. To stop erosion, we must be willing to confront our own sin, then the sin around us. An attentive parent will help his or her child recognize and correct patterns of spiritual neglect.

Take Time

How many times have you heard, "Take time with your kids"? It's still true. If we're going to weave godliness into the fabric of their lives, we have to spend hours at the loom. Eat together. Pray together. Read the Bible together. Play with your kids. Have lots of open, two-way discussions. Laugh and cry together. Get into their world, know what interests and excites them. And be around enough for them to observe your walk with God. You might even find that it will change you.

No, God doesn't have grandchildren. But he has given us the privilege and responsibility of passing along His truth to our children so that they, too, can become sons and daughters of our Father in heaven (see Deut. 6:6–9).

Living Insights

How bad do you have to be for God to give up on you? As bad as Manasseh, a child-sacrificing, idol-worshiping rebel? Worse than that, apparently, for God even gave Manasseh a second chance.

> And the Lord spoke to Manasseh and his people, but they paid no attention. Therefore the Lord brought the commanders of the army of the king of Assyria against them, and they captured Manasseh with hooks, bound him with bronze chains, and took him to Babylon. And when he was in distress, he entreated the Lord his God and humbled himself greatly before the God of his fathers. When he prayed to Him, He was moved by his entreaty and heard his supplication, and brought him again to Jerusalem to his kingdom. Then Manasseh knew that the Lord was God. (2 Chron. 33:10–13)

What a patient God we have. Most of us would have given up on Manasseh long before God did. We would have turned him over to the enemy, not for spiritual development as God did, but for destruction. We would have written him off as unreachable, unteachable, perhaps beyond the scope of God's grace.

Aren't you glad God doesn't give up on us? That He loves us enough to bring circumstances into our lives to turn us back to

Him? Can you think of a time you felt hopelessly distant from God, then found Him eagerly waiting for you when you called out to Him?

_____

_____

_____

What about right now? Do you need to be reminded of His faithful love and readiness to forgive? What do the following passages tell you about these qualities?

Psalm 103:8–14_____

_____

_____

Ezekiel 18:21–23_____

_____

_____

Luke 23:33–34 _____

_____

_____

1 Timothy 1:12–17_____

_____

_____

Whenever you feel as though you've drifted so far God will never find you, think of Manasseh. Then come back to these verses and use them as points of reconnection with your loving and patient Father. You'll find Him waiting.

Chapter 10

YOUNG, YES . . . BUT OH, SO CAPABLE!

2 Chronicles 34–35

Youth is wasted on the young" would never have come out of the mouth of Winston Churchill. He wrote,

> You will make all kinds of mistakes; but as long as you are generous and true, and also fierce, you cannot hurt the world or even seriously distress her. She was made to be wooed and won by youth.[1]

One generous and true youth who wooed and won his world for God was young King Josiah. Only eight years old when he became king, he flamed with passion for his Lord by the time he reached sixteen. And at twenty, he fiercely opposed the wickedness and idolatry that polluted the land and launched a national reform that reintroduced God's people to their God.

Josiah glitters like gold from the dark shaft of Israel's past. And his brilliant story provides a fitting end to our study of *Golden Nuggets from Forgotten Places*.

A Tarnished Heritage

You would think that character as precious as Josiah's would have been dug from a rich family vein of righteousness. But just the opposite is true. Josiah's godly reign stands in sharp contrast to the wickedness of both his grandfather and father.

Manasseh, Josiah's Grandfather

Remember Manasseh? Unlike his devout father, Hezekiah, he was the "baddest of the bad." He reinstituted idolatry—even setting up pagan altars in the Lord's temple. He sacrificed his sons in the fire, practiced witchcraft, and consulted mediums. His testimony rises from the pages of Scripture like stench from a sewer.

---

1. Sir Winston Churchill, as quoted in *Bartlett's Familiar Quotations*, 15th ed., rev. and enl., ed. Emily Morison Beck (Boston, Mass.: Little, Brown and Co., 1980), p. 743.

> And he did evil in the sight of the Lord according
> to the abominations of the nations whom the Lord
> dispossessed before the sons of Israel. . . . Thus
> Manasseh misled Judah and the inhabitants of Jerus-
> alem to do more evil than the nations whom the
> Lord destroyed before the sons of Israel.
> (2 Chron. 33:2, 9)

Except for one brief period of repentance (vv. 10–17),
Manasseh's fifty-five-year reign elevated wickedness to new heights.

Amon, Josiah's Father

Manasseh's son Amon reigned only a fraction of the time his
father did—two years—but his wickedness was just as great.

> And he did evil in the sight of the Lord as Manasseh
> his father had done, and Amon sacrificed to all the
> carved images which his father Manasseh had made,
> and he served them. Moreover, he did not humble
> himself before the Lord as his father Manasseh had
> done, but Amon multiplied guilt. (vv. 22–23)

As if that's not enough scandal, Amon was murdered in his own
house by his own servants. After the people of Judah dealt with
the conspirators, they made Josiah king.

Two Excuses We Need to Ignore

Wickedness. Witchcraft. Idolatry. Conspiracy. Murder. Some
heritage! Could a decent, normal child emerge from such a spiritual
cesspool? Josiah did, even earning this rarely given banner over his
life: "He did right in the sight of the Lord" (34:2). And he was so
young. He made more of an impact by his late teens and early
twenties than most of us make in a lifetime. Josiah's story refutes
at least two common excuses heard today for spiritual ineffectiveness.

1. *"Young people can't really make a difference."* Who says you have
to have gray hair (or no hair) and a mile-long resumé to make a difference for God? Certainly not Scripture. Josiah, as we've seen, was just
a youth. God called Samuel when he was just a boy serving under Eli
(1 Sam. 3). And David was younger than all his warrior-brothers
when he killed Goliath (chap. 17). Likewise, Timothy was so much
younger than the rest of the Christians at Ephesus that Paul had to remind him, "Let no one look down on your youthfulness" (1 Tim. 4:12).

Yes, age and experience are valuable. But we can't count others out just because they're young. After all, it's the heart that matters most to God, regardless of the age of the body that surrounds it.

2. *"A troubled family background disqualifies you from making any significant contributions."* Our upbringing does shape our personalities and values, yet we can overcome negative influences with God's grace. Though Josiah had only the fifty-seven-year legacy of two godless and idolatrous kings—a dysfunctional family if there ever was one—he still followed the Lord. That's fresh hope for all who feel that past problems disqualify them from serving the Lord.

One Man We Can't Help Respecting

Let's take a closer look at Josiah's life and the impact he made on Judah.

What He Did . . . and When

Verses 3–7 of 2 Chronicles 34 describe two ages and stages of Josiah's life. We're told, first of all, that

> in the eighth year of his reign while he was still a
> youth, he began to seek the God of his father David.
> (v. 3a)

Throughout Kings and Chronicles, David is held up as the standard of a godly king, one who followed God with his whole heart. So Josiah's association with David's devotion is no coincidence. Josiah sought the Lord, just as David had before him. *Seek* is a word of deliberate pursuit. Its various translations include "to search carefully," "to inquire," and "to study." By the time he was sixteen years old, Josiah had made a decision to make learning about the living God his top priority.

Talk about resisting peer pressure! After fifty-seven years of wicked and idolatrous leadership, how many people do you think urged sixteen-year-old Josiah to pursue God? Probably a few, but not many.

This conscious quest to know God enabled Josiah to reform Judah. A rich relationship with the Lord always precedes great accomplishments for Him. For example, before Jesus sent out the disciples to preach, He assembled them "that they might be with Him" (Mark 3:14). In our society, though, we're often more interested in doing than being. We want to accomplish great things

81

for God—build churches, develop programs, reform politics—without first letting Him do His work in us. Before we ask, "What does God want me to do?" we should be asking, "Am I seeking God?" What did Josiah's relationship with God accomplish?

> In the twelfth year he began to purge Judah and Jerusalem of the high places, the Asherim, the carved images, and the molten images. And they tore down the altars of the Baals in his presence, and the incense altars that were high above them he chopped down; also the Asherim, the carved images, and the molten images he broke in pieces and ground to powder and scattered it on the graves of those who had sacrificed to them. Then he burned the bones of the priests on their altars, and purged Judah and Jerusalem. And in the cities of Manasseh, Ephraim, Simeon, even as far as Naphtali, in their surrounding ruins, he also tore down the altars and beat the Asherim and the carved images into powder, and chopped down all the incense altars throughout the land of Israel. Then he returned to Jerusalem. (2 Chron. 34:3b–7)

In his efforts to purge Judah of idolatry, King Josiah, "broke down the high places of the gates" (2 Kings 23:8). This reconstructed sanctuary at Tel Arad in southern Israel is representative of the high places Josiah destroyed during his reforms.

Amazingly, Josiah did all this without a completed copy of the Scriptures in front of him. Alexander Whyte explains that

> the whole of that immense movement that resulted in the religious regeneration of Jerusalem and Judah in Josiah's day,—it all sprang originally and immediately out of nothing else but Josiah's extraordinary tenderness of heart. The Light that lighteth every man that cometh into the world shone with extraordinary clearness in Josiah's tender heart and open mind. And Josiah walked in that Light and obeyed it, till it became within him an overmastering sense of divine duty and an irresistible direction and drawing of the Divine Hand.[2]

Why He Did It . . . and How

Why did Josiah follow God instead of walking in the wayward footsteps of his father and grandfather? Scripture suggests three reasons.

First, a godly mother. Josiah's mother receives only brief mention in 2 Kings 22:

> His mother's name was Jedidah the daughter of Adaiah of Bozkath. (v. 1b)

Interestingly, her name comes between the mention of Josiah's reign (v. 1) and his doing right in God's sight and walking "in all the way of his father David" (v. 2), which may imply her influence. We're not told how Josiah spent his first eight years on the throne (prior to his beginning to seek the Lord at sixteen), but it's possible that Jedidah provided a godly influence during that time.

Second, an open Bible. As mentioned earlier, Josiah had no copy of the Scriptures when he started his reform at twenty years of age. But later in his reign, when he was about twenty-six, he ordered the repair of the Lord's temple. During renovation, a priest discovered a long-lost treasure—the dusty scrolls containing the books of the Law that God had given to Moses. Take a look at how Josiah responded when he heard God's Word.

---

2. Alexander Whyte, *Bible Characters* (1952; reprint, London, England: Oliphants, 1959), vol. 1, p. 359.

Moreover, Shaphan the scribe told the king saying, "Hilkiah the priest gave me a book." And Shaphan read from it in the presence of the king. And it came about when the king heard the words of the law that he tore his clothes. (2 Chron. 34:18–19)

Josiah grieved over his nation's disregard for the commandments of God (vv. 20–21). He honored and revered the Word. You want to influence your generation? You want to be a light in the darkness? Then follow God's Word.

Third, a tender heart. Josiah wanted more information about the Law of God, particularly how God might judge Judah for their disobedience (v. 21). So the king's priest went to Huldah the prophetess, who revealed the certainty of God's coming judgment (vv. 23–25). But she also disclosed that Josiah would be spared the misery of God's wrath.

> ""Because your heart was tender and you humbled yourself before God, when you heard His words against this place and against its inhabitants, and because you humbled yourself before Me, tore your clothes, and wept before Me, I truly have heard you," declares the Lord.'" (v. 27)

Josiah's tender heart, which kept him open to God's leading, also spared him from God's judgment.

The text doesn't list the specific characteristics of a tender heart, but here are four signs that usually indicate one:

1. A respect for God's truth. Only a hard heart rejects the Word or reads it without being affected.

2. A genuine fear of God. This means more than a casual relationship. A heart malleable before God is a humble one—brimming with awe and reverence for its Creator.

3. A willingness to change. Josiah responded to the Law by making a covenant with God to keep His commandments (v. 31). That's how we need to respond to the truth we discover in Scripture— with a firm resolve to follow God in all He commands.

4. A strong commitment to God's standard of holiness. A passion for holiness means dealing radically with sin, getting rid of anything and everything that hinders our walk with God (v. 33).

Josiah was serious about keeping the Word of the Lord. He reinstated the Passover, complete with the priestly order and practices (35:1–19). And he led the people in worshiping the Lord.

> And there had not been celebrated a Passover like it in Israel since the days of Samuel the prophet; nor had any of the kings of Israel celebrated such a Passover as Josiah did with the priests, the Levites, all Judah and Israel who were present, and the inhabitants of Jerusalem. (v. 18)

Where He Died . . . and How He's Remembered

Josiah died in battle against Neco, king of Egypt, at the age of thirty-nine. A short life? By some standards, yes. But he lived long enough to open the spiritual blinds of Judah and let the holiness of God inside.

The country he enlightened mourned his loss (v. 24). The prophet Jeremiah chanted a lament for the king, a eulogy continued by singers long after Josiah's death (v. 25). And notice what stood out about his life:

> Now the rest of the acts of Josiah and *his deeds of devotion* as written in the law of the Lord, and his acts, first to last, behold, they are written in the Book of the Kings of Israel and Judah. (vv. 26–27, emphasis added)

His deeds of devotion. Not his money, his title, his fame, or his political savvy. When we live a life that honors God, what we do for Him will outlive all else.

Epilogue

Judah, like Israel, was eventually judged for her years of wickedness. Jerusalem was invaded and her inhabitants enslaved by the Babylonians in 586 B.C. But even among the exiles, there were those whom God preserved as His true representatives. A reminder that true godliness thrives in any environment.

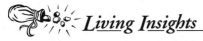 *Living Insights*

"If only my parents had taught me about God."

"If we had a better preacher, I know I could grow."

"How do you expect me to make a difference in a world that's coming apart at the seams?"

"It's no use; standing up for God is too hard, too risky."

Had Josiah fallen into the trap of making such excuses, he may have been just another name on a list of corrupt kings. But his God was more influential than his past, bigger than his environment, stronger than the opposition.

That doesn't mean he was unaware of the negative influences around him, nor should we be. God never asks us to abandon reality, to live in denial of our problems or past, or to pretend that following Him is always easy. In the midst of the struggle, however, He wants to be our inexhaustible source of strength and sufficiency.

Is He that for you? Spend some time in the following verses. Let them remind you of His nearness, His power, and His faithfulness.

Deuteronomy 31:1–8 _____

_____

Psalm 3 _____

_____

Psalm 46:1–3_____

_____

Matthew 7:7–11 _____

_____

Ephesians 6:10–20 _____

_____

1 John 4:4 _____

_____

Digging Deeper

Thanks for joining us in digging around these "forgotten places." Now that you have a whole sack full of golden nuggets, which lessons seem most pertinent to you at this point in your life?

_____

_____

_____

What changes have you made, or can you make, as a result of what you've learned? Specifically, what can you work on over the next few weeks?

_____

_____

_____

Into what topics or passages would you like to dig more deeply? Do you need to plan your own study right now?

_____

_____

_____

_____

_____

_____

_____

_____

Remember, though we've unearthed a few shining nuggets, there's infinite treasure to be found in God's Word. So never stop digging. The deeper you go, the deeper you'll grow. Happy mining!

BOOKS FOR
PROBING FURTHER

Want to know more about Israel's history? Or take a deeper look into the hearts of Judah's kings? Maybe you would like to learn more about how to be a leader from godly kings and prophets (or how *not* to lead from ungodly ones). If so, peruse the following list and consider adding a few of these books to your study shelf.

Blaiklock, E. M. *Today's Handbook of Bible Characters.* Minneapolis, Minn.: Bethany House Publishers, 1979.

Bright, John. *A History of Israel.* 3d ed. Philadelphia, Pa.: Westminster Press, 1981.

Keller, W. Phillip. *David I: The Time of Saul's Tyranny.* Waco, Tex.: Word Books, 1985.

————. *David II: The Shepherd King.* Waco, Tex.: Word Books, 1986.

Walvoord, John F., and Roy B. Zuck, eds., *The Bible Knowledge Commentary.* Old Testament edition. Wheaton, Ill.: Scripture Press Publications, Victor Books, 1985.

Whyte, Alexander. *Bible Characters from the Old and New Testaments.* 1896. Reprint, with a new introduction, Grand Rapids, Mich.: Kregel Publications, 1990.

Wilcock, Michael. *The Message of Chronicles: One Church, One Faith, One Lord.* The Bible Speaks Today series. Downers Grove, Ill.: InterVarsity Press, 1987.

Wiseman, Donald J. *1 and 2 Kings: An Introduction and Commentary.* Downers Grove, Ill.: InterVarsity Press, 1993.

Some of these books may be out of print and available only through a library. For those currently available, please contact your local Christian bookstore. Books by Charles R. Swindoll may be obtained through Insight for Living. IFL also offers some books by other authors—please note the ordering information that follows and contact the office that serves you.

Acknowledgments

Insight for Living is grateful to the sources below for permission to use their material.

All photos are from the personal collection of Gordon Franz.

The illustration on page 48 of the priest with the censer is from Frank H. White, *Panorama of the Tabernacle*. No date, no publisher.

ORDERING INFORMATION

GOLDEN NUGGETS FROM FORGOTTEN PLACES
Cassette Tapes and Study Guide

This Bible study guide was designed to be used independently or in conjunction with the broadcast of Chuck Swindoll's taped messages which are listed below. If you would like to order cassette tapes or further copies of this study guide, please see the information given below and the order forms provided at the end of this guide.

		U.S.	Canada
GNF	Study guide	$ 4.95 ea.	$ 6.50 ea.
GNFCS	Cassette series, includes all individual tapes, album cover, and one complimentary study guide	34.75 ea.	40.75 ea.
GNF 1–5	Individual cassettes, includes messages A and B	6.00 ea.	7.48 ea.

Prices are subject to change without notice.

GNF 1-A: *Dig . . . and You Shall Find*—A Historical Survey of Kings and Chronicles
    B: *Praise God from Whom All Blessings Flow*— 1 Chronicles 29:1–22

GNF 2-A: *Erosion: It Starts at the Top*—1 Kings 14; 2 Chronicles 10–12
    B: *The Benefits of Godly, Gutsy Counsel*—2 Chronicles 15

GNF 3-A: *It All Starts with the Heart*—2 Chronicles 15–16
    B: *Warnings for All in Leadership*—2 Chronicles 26

GNF 4-A: *The Exit of a Nation*—2 Kings 17
    B: *Just a Chunk of Bronze*—2 Kings 18:1–4; Numbers 21:4–9

GNF 5-A: *Like Father, Like Son?*—2 Kings 21; 2 Chronicles 33
    B: *Young, Yes . . . but Oh, So Capable!*— 2 Chronicles 34–35

HOW TO ORDER BY PHONE OR FAX
(Credit card orders only)

Internet address: http://www.insight.org

United States: 1-800-772-8888 or FAX (714) 575-5684, 24 hours a day, 7 days a week

Canada: 1-800-663-7639. Vancouver residents call (604) 532-7172, from 8:00 A.M. to 4:30 P.M., Pacific time, Monday through Friday FAX (604) 532-7173 anytime, day or night

Australia and the South Pacific: (03) 9872-4606 or FAX (03) 9874-8890 from 8:00 A.M. to 5:00 P.M., Monday through Friday

Other International Locations: call the International Ordering Services Department in the United States at (714) 575-5000 from 8:00 A.M. to 4:30 P.M., Pacific time, Monday through Friday FAX (714) 575-5683 anytime, day or night

HOW TO ORDER BY MAIL

United States
- Mail to: Mail Center
  Insight for Living
  Post Office Box 69000
  Anaheim, CA 92817-0900
- Sales tax: California residents add 7.25%.
- Shipping and handling charges must be added to each order. See chart on order form for amount.
- Payment: personal checks, money orders, credit cards (Visa, Master-Card, Discover Card, and American Express). No invoices or COD orders available.
- $10 fee for *any* returned check.

Canada
- Mail to: Insight for Living Ministries
  Post Office Box 2510
  Vancouver, BC V6B 3W7
- Sales tax: please add 7% GST. British Columbia residents also add 7% sales tax (on tapes or cassette series).
- Shipping and handling charges must be added to each order. See chart on order form for amount.
- Payment: personal cheques, money orders, credit cards (Visa, Master-Card). No invoices or COD orders available.
- Delivery: approximately four weeks.

Australia and the South Pacific
- Mail to: Insight for Living, Inc.
  GPO Box 2823 EE
  Melbourne, Victoria 3001, Australia
- Shipping: add 25% to the total order.
- Delivery: approximately four to six weeks.
- Payment: personal cheques payable in Australian funds, international money orders, or credit cards (Visa, MasterCard, and Bankcard).

United Kingdom and Europe
- Mail to: Insight for Living
  c/o Trans World Radio
  Post Office Box 1020
  Bristol, BS99 1XS
  England, United Kingdom
- Shipping: add 25% to the total order.
- Delivery: approximately four to six weeks.
- Payment: cheques payable in sterling pounds or credit cards (Visa, MasterCard, and American Express).

Other International Locations
- Mail to: International Processing Services Department
  Insight for Living
  Post Office Box 69000
  Anaheim, CA 92817-0900
- Shipping and delivery time: please see chart that follows.
- Payment: personal checks payable in U.S. funds, international money orders, or credit cards (Visa, MasterCard, and American Express).

Type of Shipping	Postage Cost	Delivery
Surface	10% of total order*	6 to 10 weeks
Airmail	25% of total order*	under 6 weeks

*Use U.S. price as a base.

Our Guarantee: Your complete satisfaction is our top priority here at Insight for Living. If you're not completely satisfied with anything you order, please return it for full credit, a refund, or a replacement, as you prefer.

Insight for Living Catalog: The Insight for Living catalog features study guides, tapes, and books by a variety of Christian authors. To obtain a free copy, call us at the numbers listed above.

Order Form
United States, Australia, and Other International Locations
(Canadian residents please use order form on reverse side.)

GNFCS represents the entire *Golden Nuggets from Fotgotten Places* series in a special album cover, while GNF 1–5 are the individual tapes included in the series. GNF represents this study guide, should you desire to order additional copies.

Product Code	Product Description	Qty.	Price	Total
GNF	Study Guide		$ 4.95	$
GNFCS	Casette Series with study guide		34.75	
GNF-	Individual cassette		6.00	
GNF-	Individual cassette		6.00	
GNF-	Individual cassette		6.00	

Subtotal

Amount of Order	First Class	UPS
$ 7.50 and under	1.00	4.00
$ 7.51 to 12.50	1.50	4.25
$12.51 to 25.00	3.50	4.50
$25.01 to 35.00	4.50	4.75
$35.01 to 60.00	5.50	5.25
$60.00 to 99.99	6.50	5.75
$100.00 and over	**No Charge**	

Rush shipping and Fourth Class are also available. Please call for details.

California Residents—Sales Tax
Add 7.75% of subtotal.

UPS ❏ **First Class** ❏
Shipping and handling must be added.
See chart for charges.

Non-United States Residents
Australia and Europe: add 25%.
Other: Price +10% surface or 25% airmail.
Gift to Insight for Living
Tax-deductible in the United States.

Total Amount Due $
Please do not send cash.

Prices are subject to change without notice.

Payment by: ❏ Check or money order payable to Insight for Living or
❏ Visa ❏ MasterCard ❏ Discover Card ❏ American Express ❏ Bankcard
(In Australia)

Number

Expiration Date ___/___ Signature
We cannot process your credit card purchase without your signature

Name:

Address:

City: State:

Zip Code: Country:

Telephone: ( ) – Radio Station:

If questions arise concerning your order, we may need to contact you.

Mail this order form to the Mail Center at one of these addresses:

Insight for Living
Post Office Box 69000, Anaheim, CA 92817-0900

Insight for Living, Inc.
GPO Box 2823 EE, Melbourne, VIC 3001, Australia

Order Form
Canadian Residents
(Residents of the United States, Australia, and other international locations, please use order form on reverse side.)

GNFCS represents the entire *Golden Nuggets from Fotgotten Places* series in a special album cover, while GNF 1–5 are the individual tapes included in the series. GNF represents this study guide, should you desire to order additional copies

Product Code	Product Description	Qty.	Price	Total
GNF	Study Guide		$ 6.50	$
GNFCS	Casette Series with study guide		40.75	
GNF-	Individual cassette		7.48	
GNF-	Individual cassette		7.48	
GNF-	Individual cassette		7.48	

Subtotal

Add 7% GST

British Columbia Residents
Add 7% sales tax on individual tapes or cassette series.

Shipping
Shipping and Handling must be added. See chart for charges.

Gift to Insight for Living Ministries
Tax-deductible in Canada.

Total Amount Due $
Please do not send cash.

Amount of Order	Canada Post
Orders to $10.00	2.00
$10.01 to 30.00	3.50
$30.01 to 50.00	5.00
$50.01 to 99.99	7.00
$100 and over	No charge

Loomis Courier is also available. Please call for details.

Prices are subject to change without notice.

Payment by: ❑ Cheque or money order payable to Insight for Living Ministries or ❑ Visa ❑ MasterCard

Number

Expiration Date ___/___ Signature

We cannot process your credit card purchase without your signature.

Name:

Address:

City: Province:

Postal Code: Country:

Telephone: ( ) − Radio Station:

If questions arise concerning your order, we may need to contact you.

Mail this order form to the Processing Services Department at the following address:

Insight for Living Ministries
Post Office Box 2510
Vancouver, BC, Canada V6B 3W7